Walt Disney's

MICKEY & FRIENDS

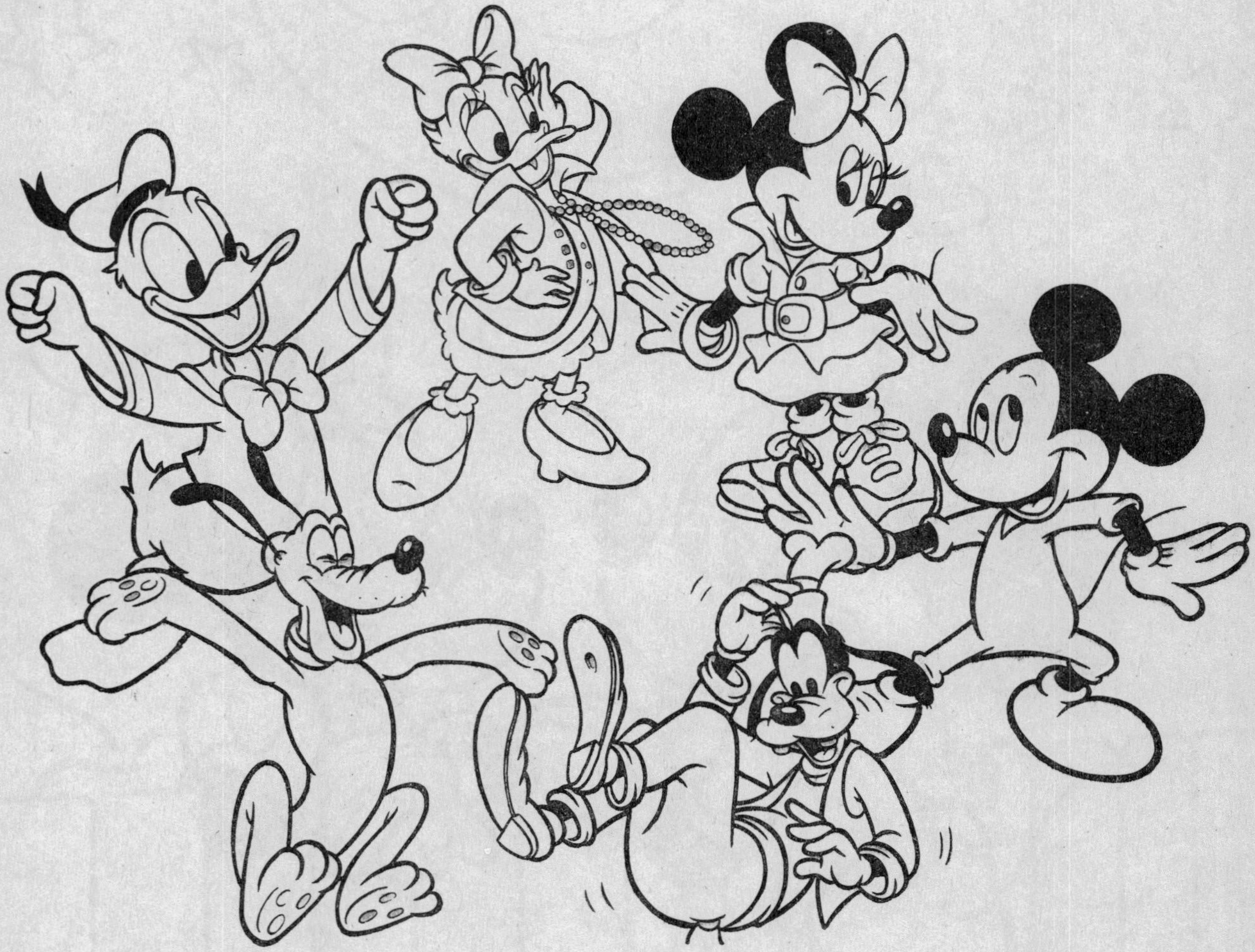

A GOLDEN BOOK®
Golden Books Publishing Company, Inc.
New York, New York 10106

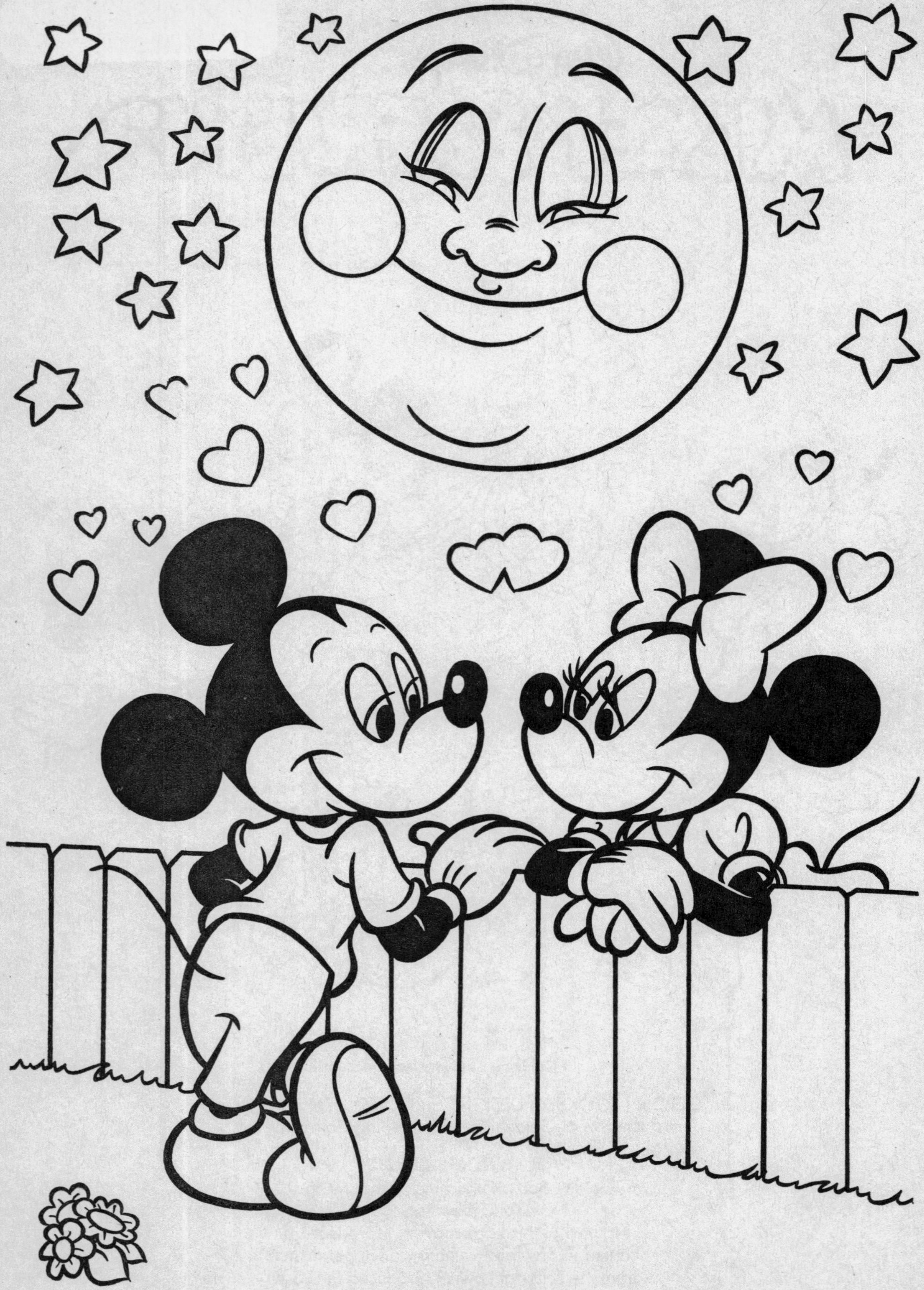

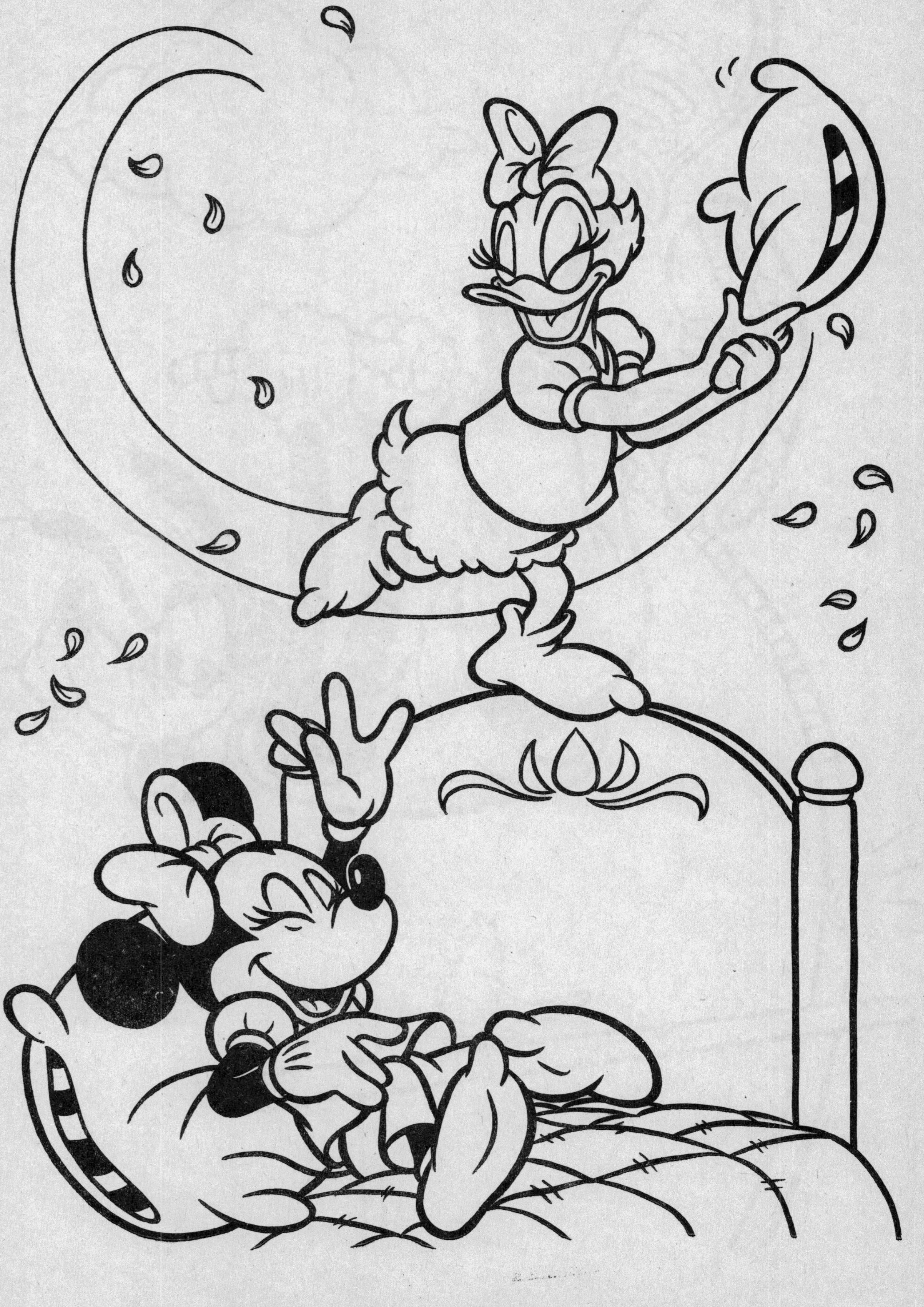

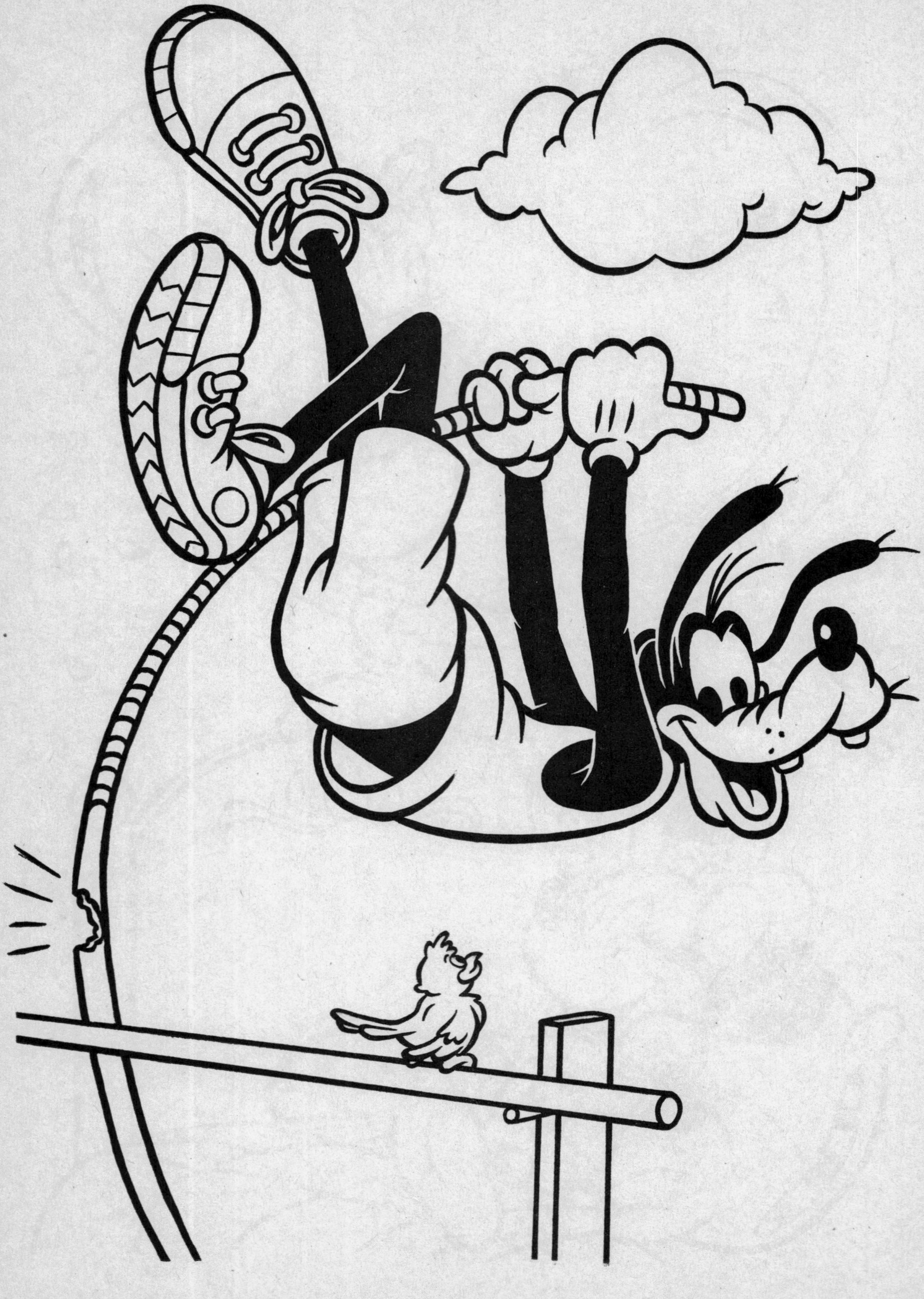

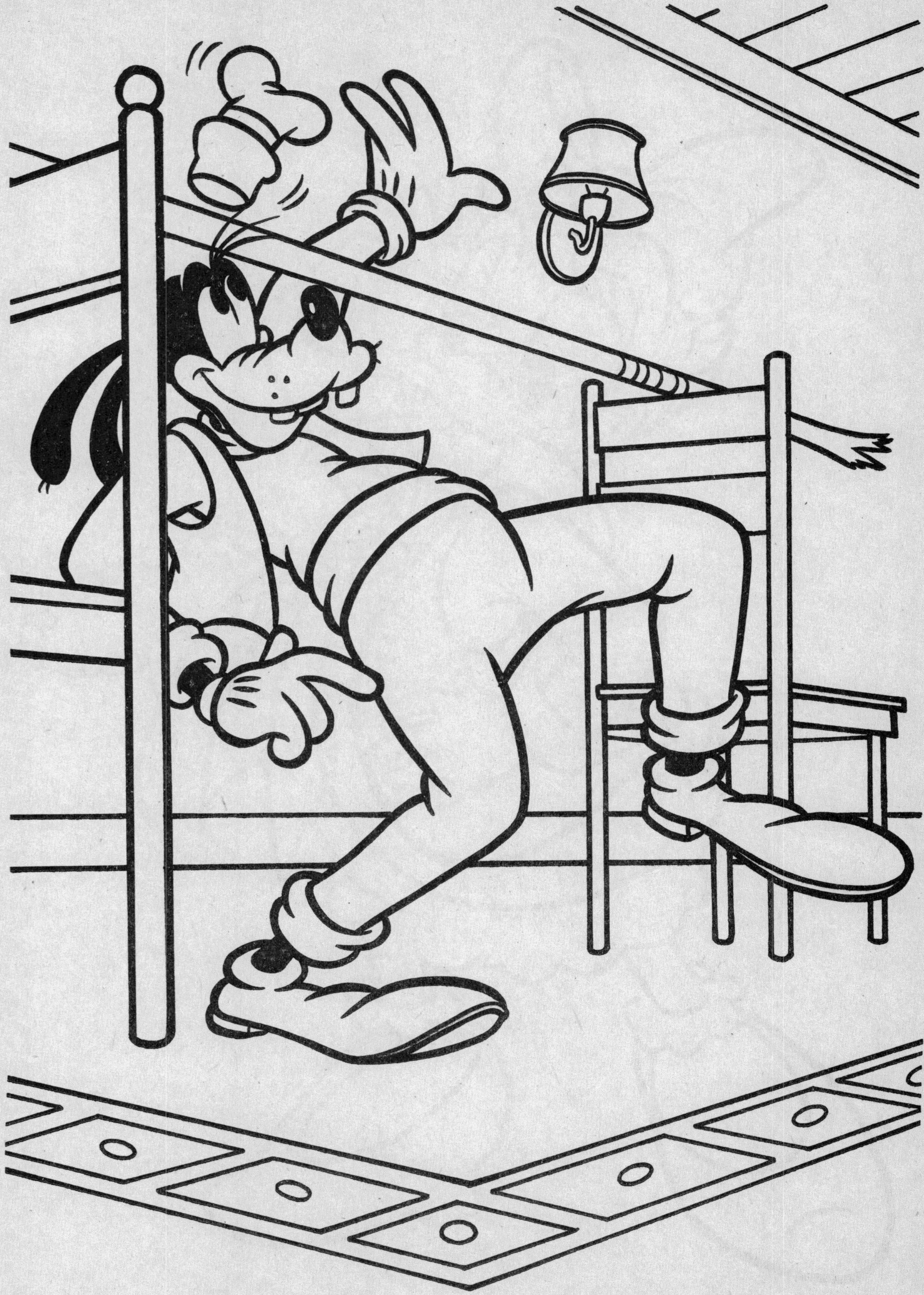

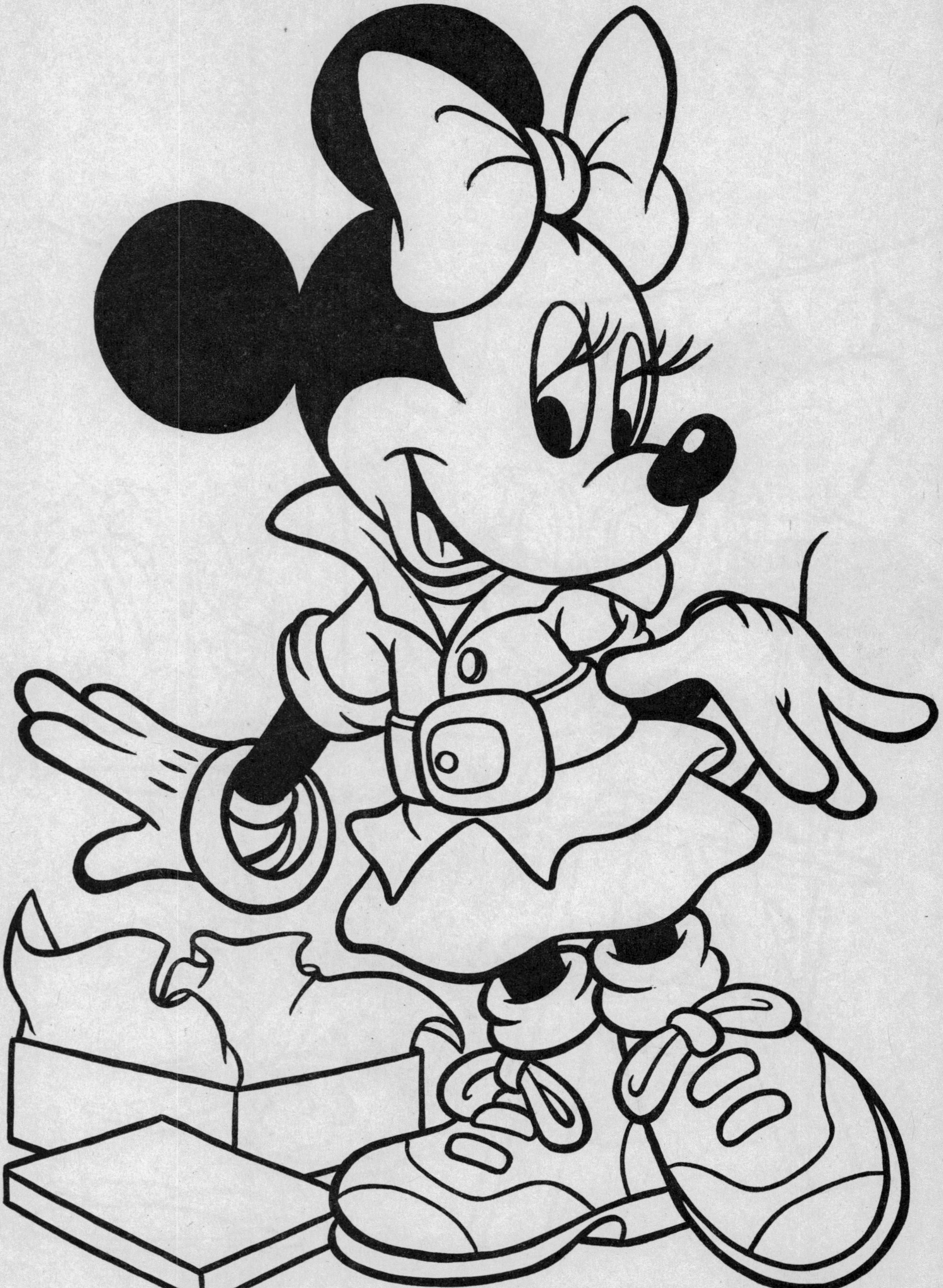

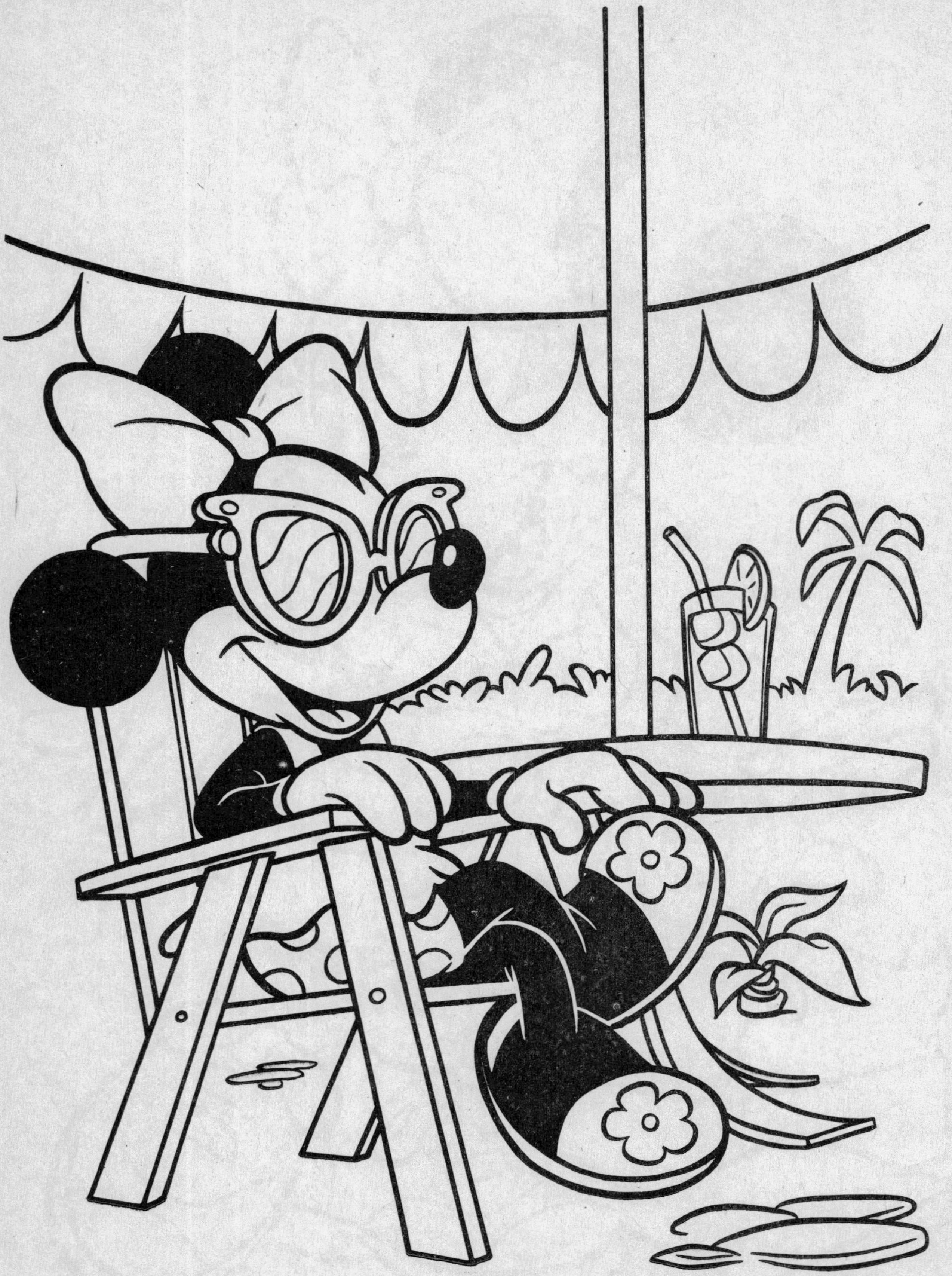

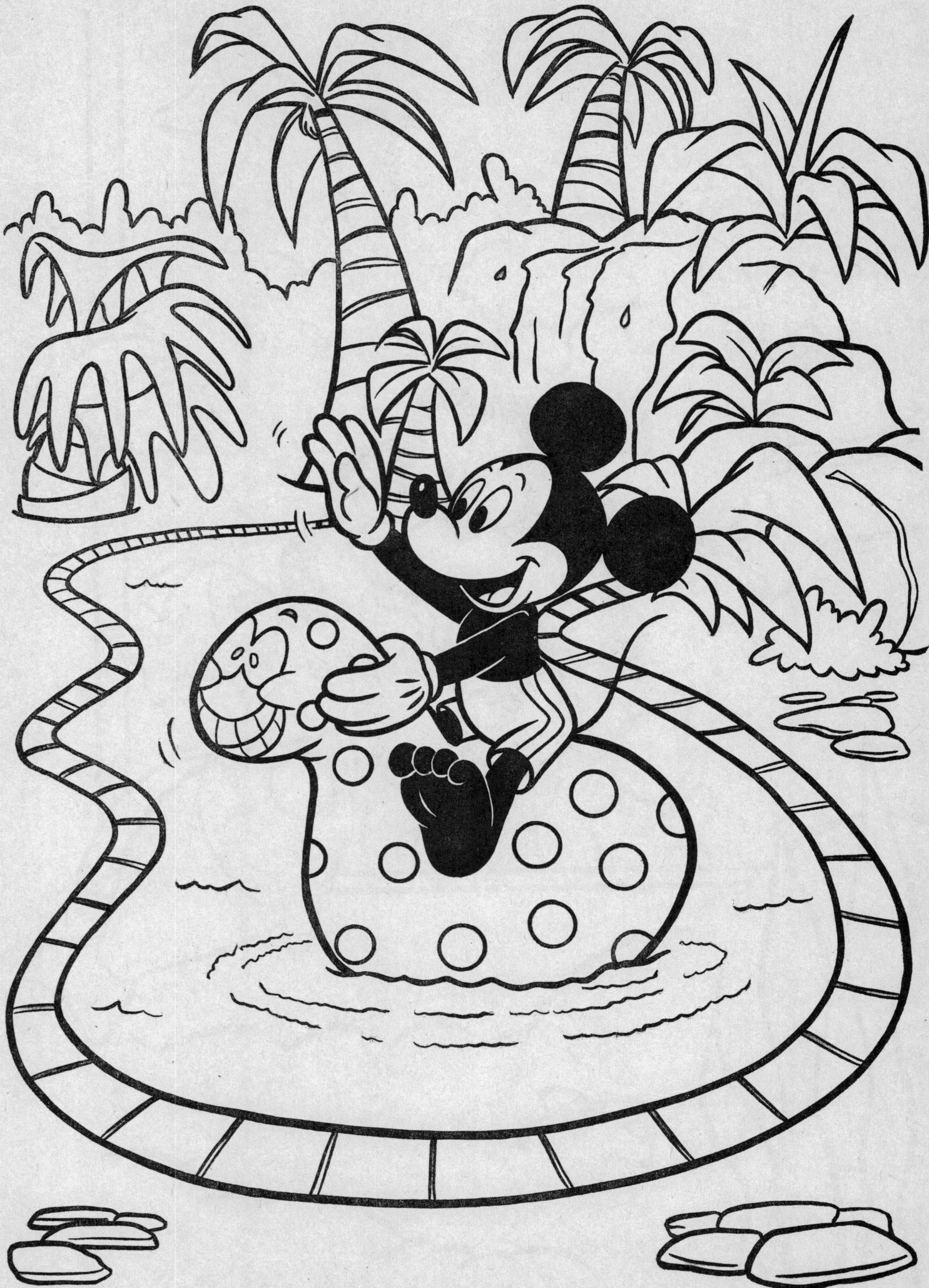

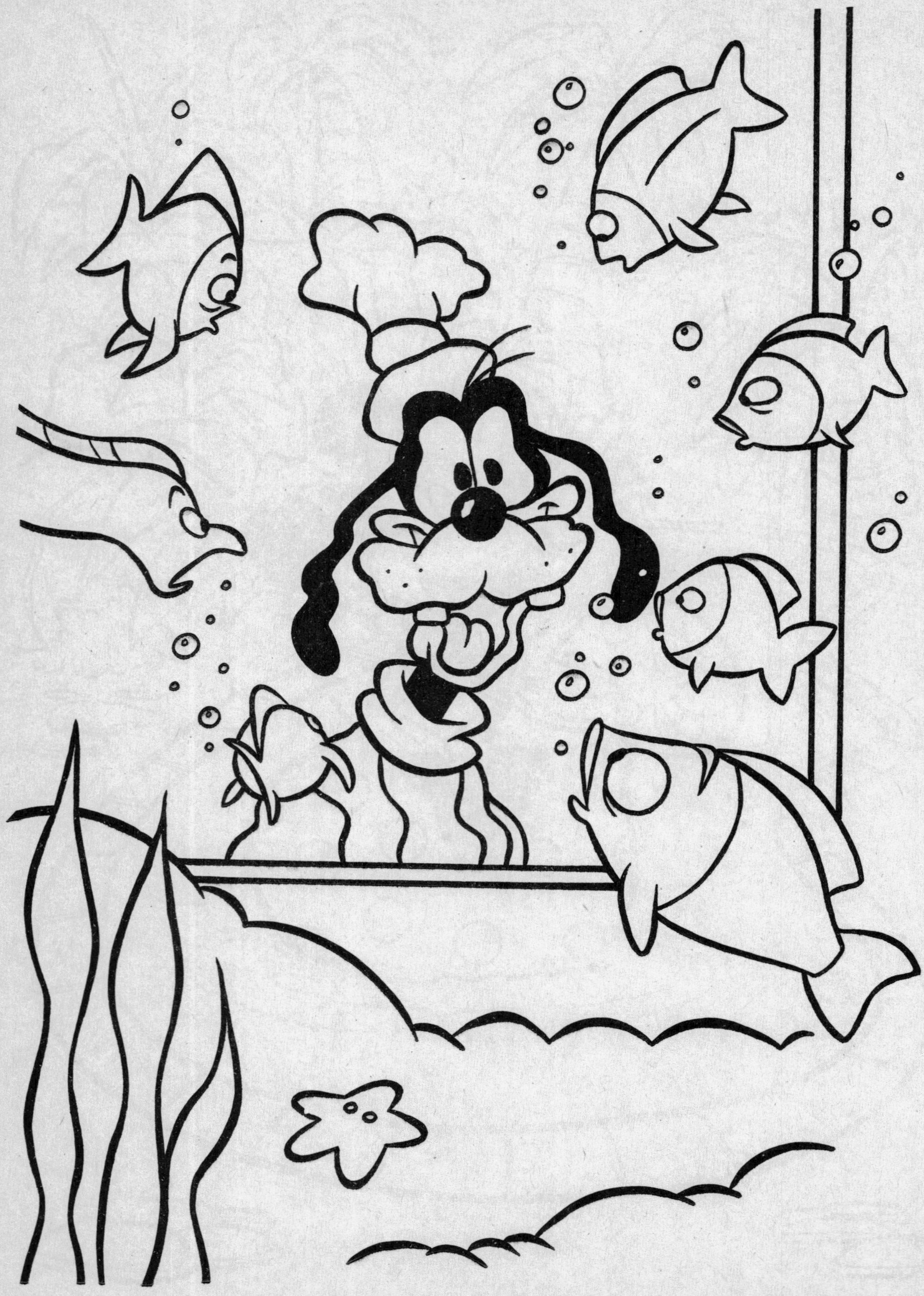

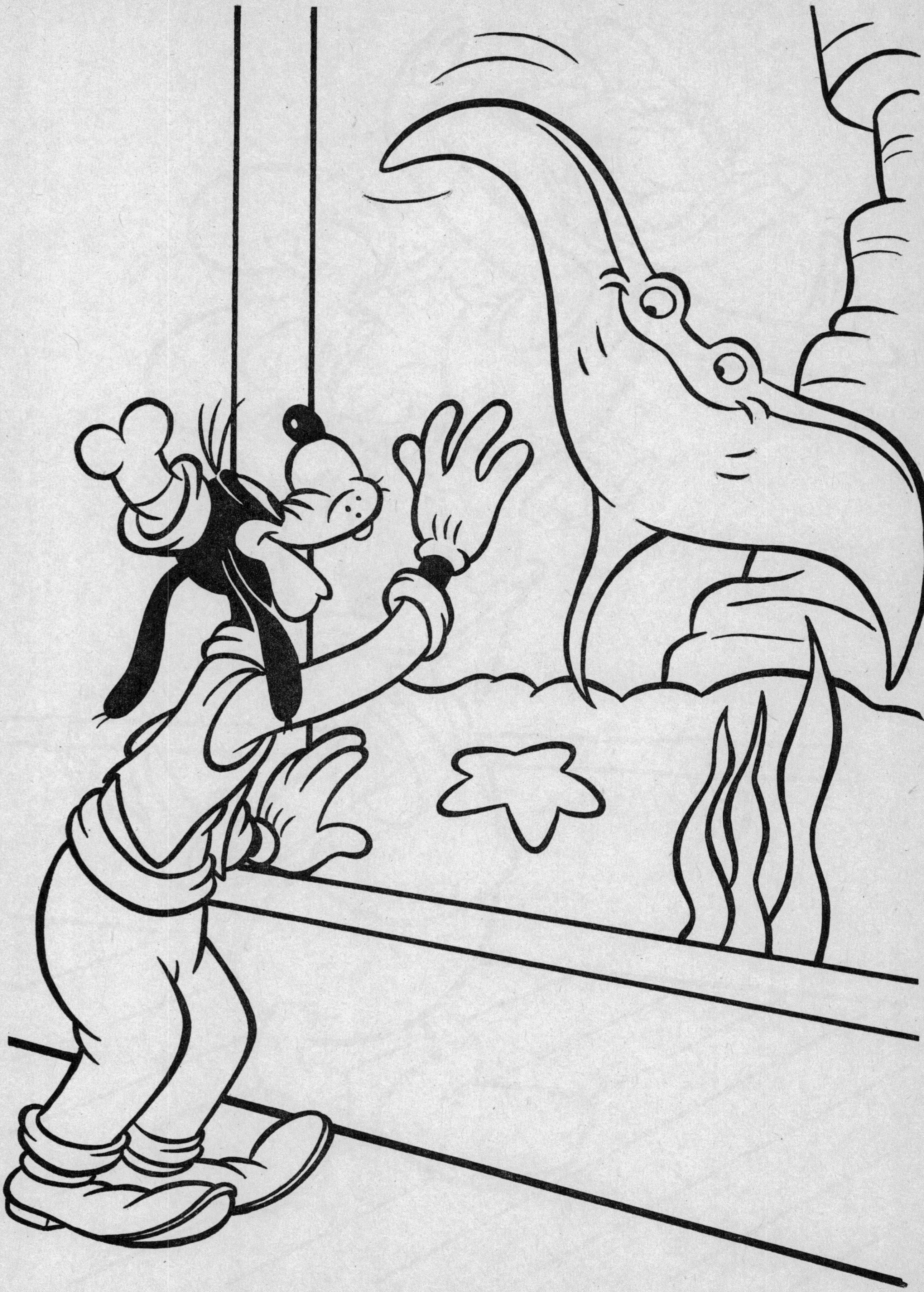

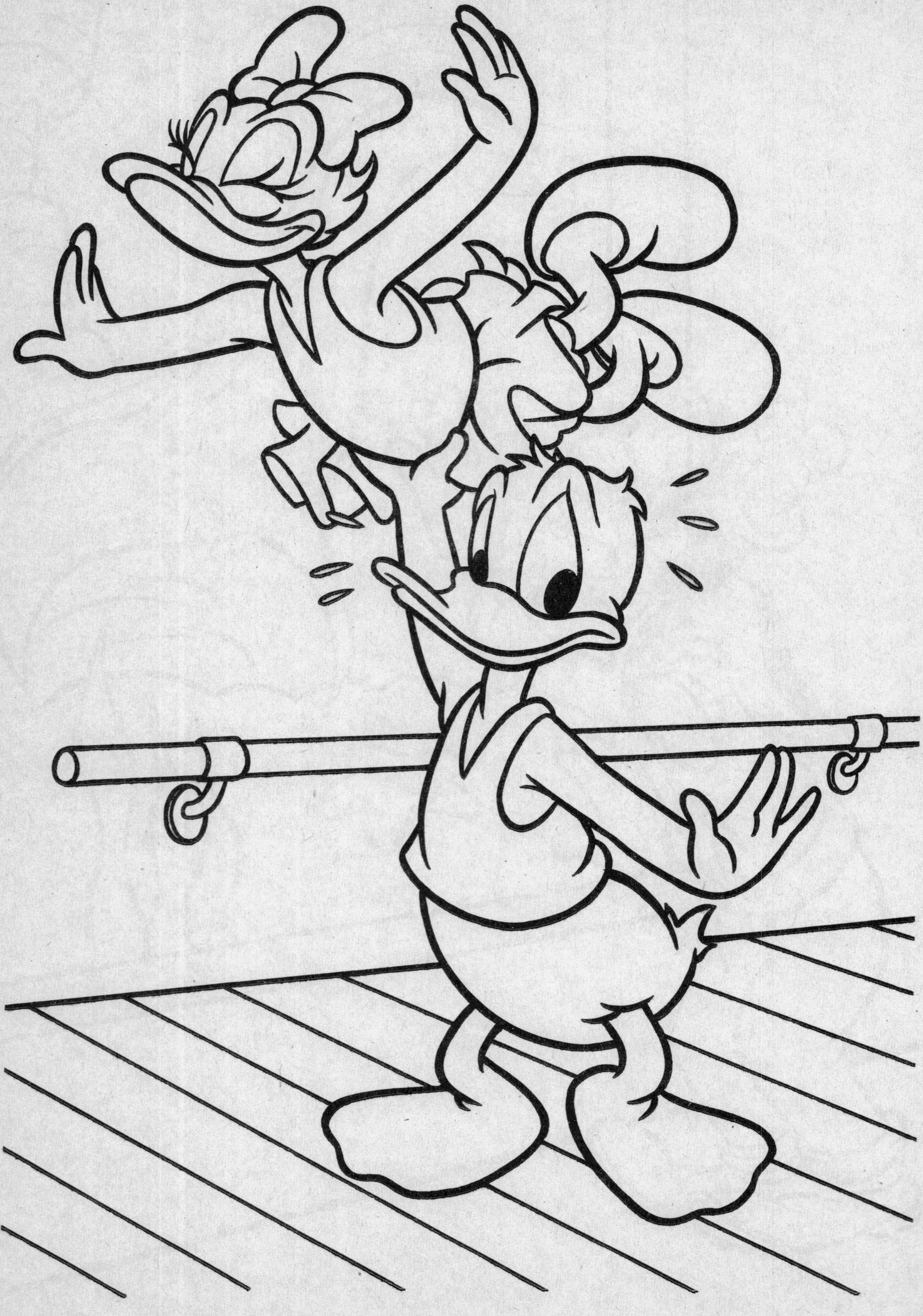

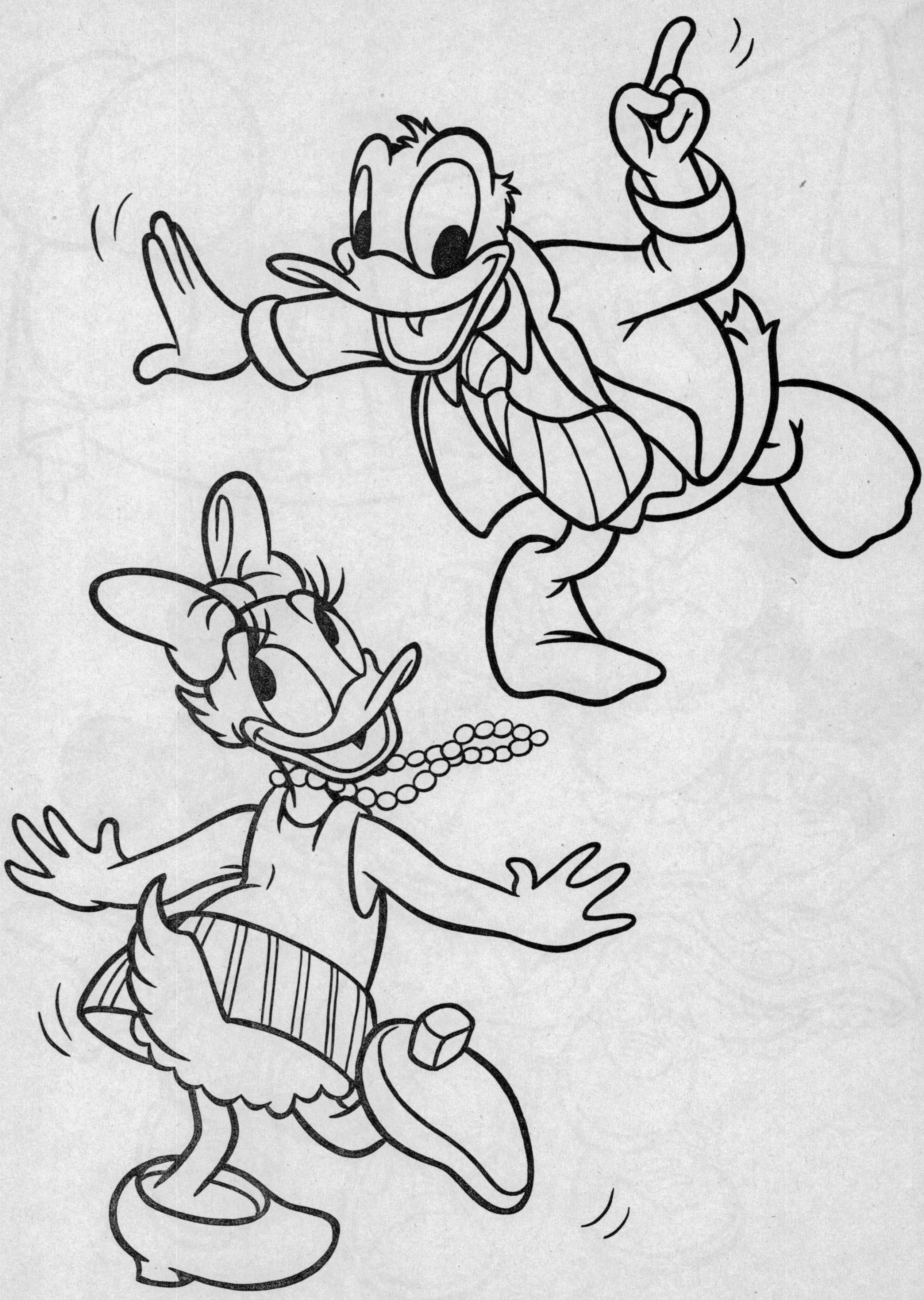

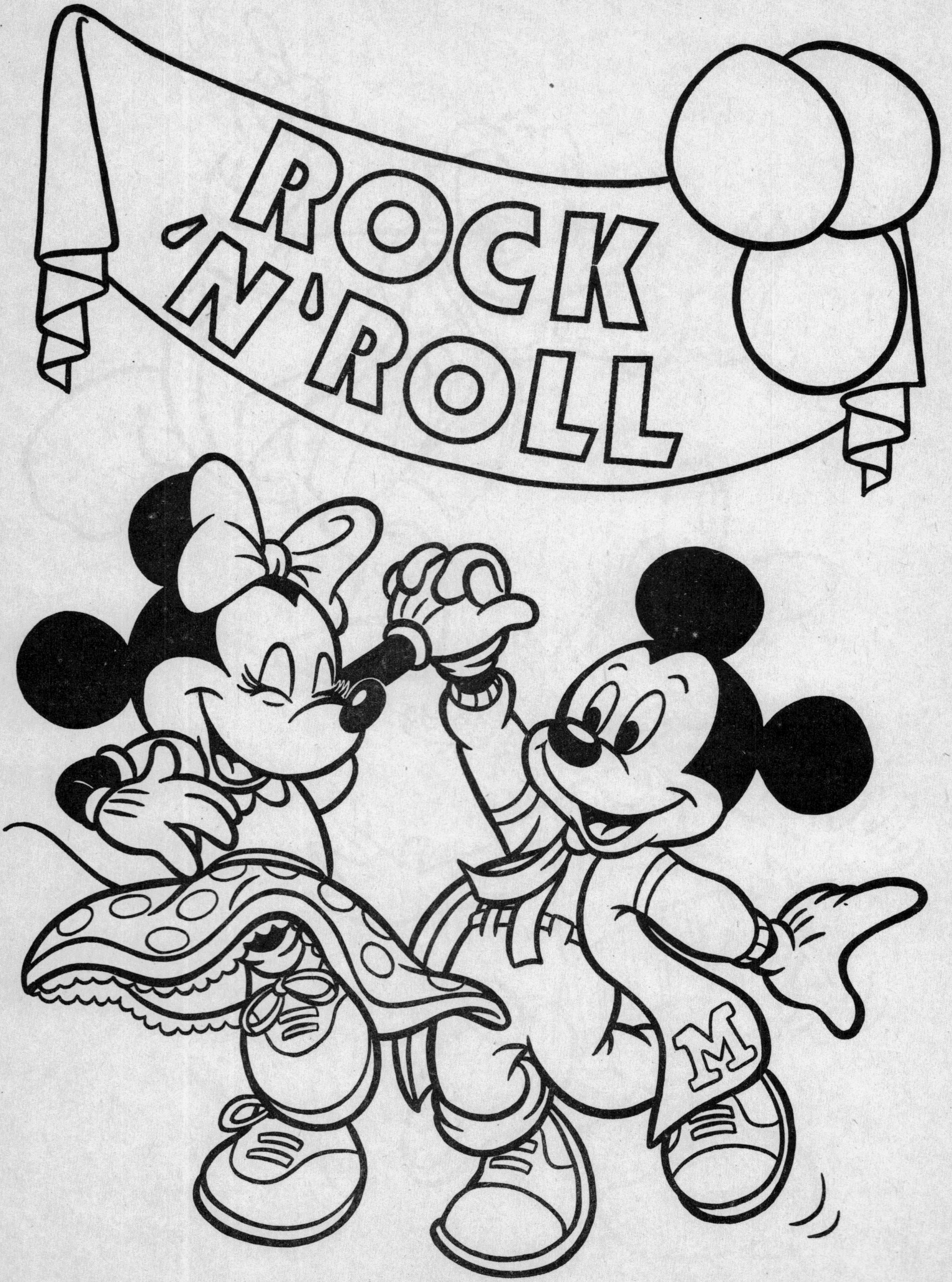
ROCK 'N' ROLL

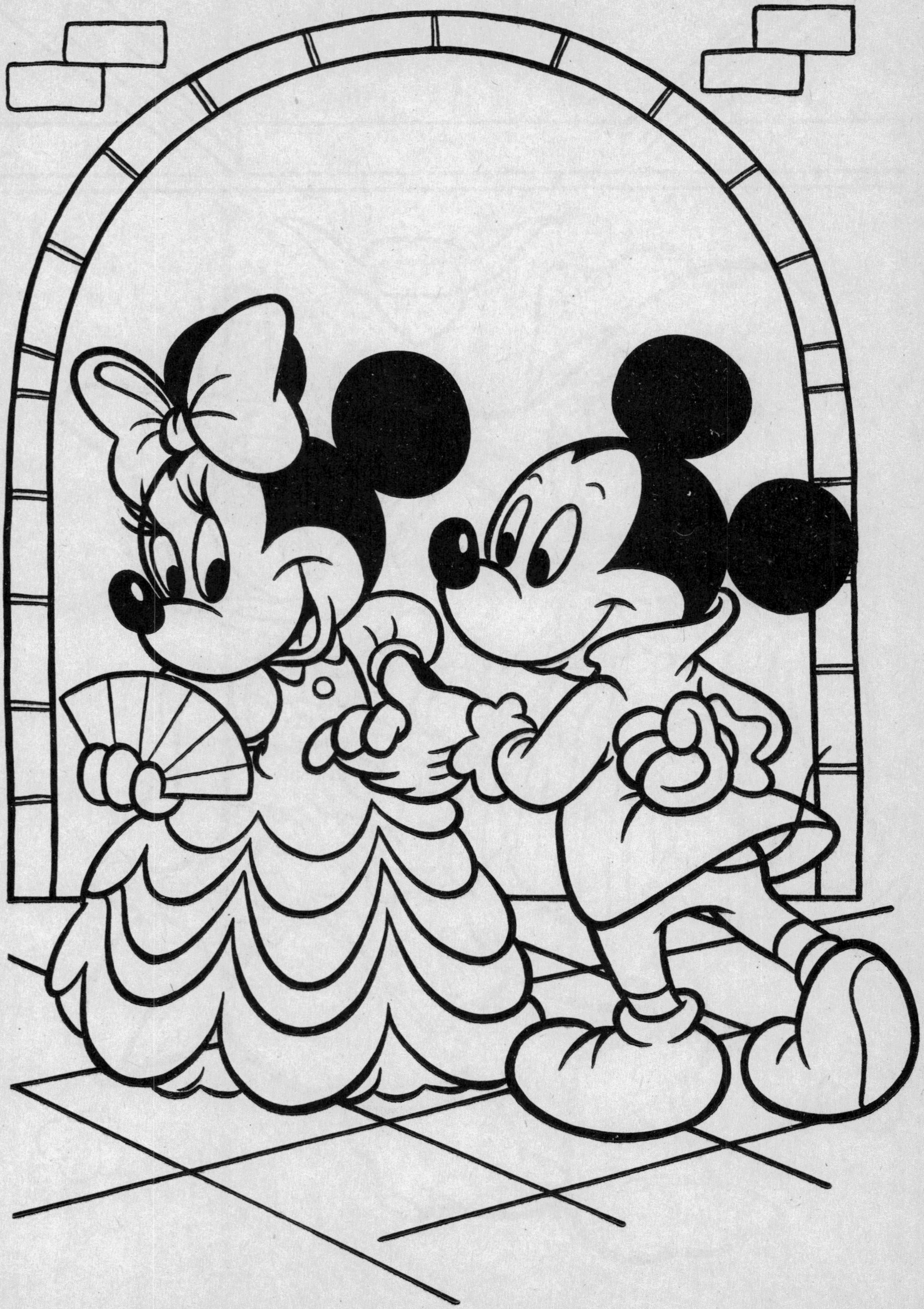

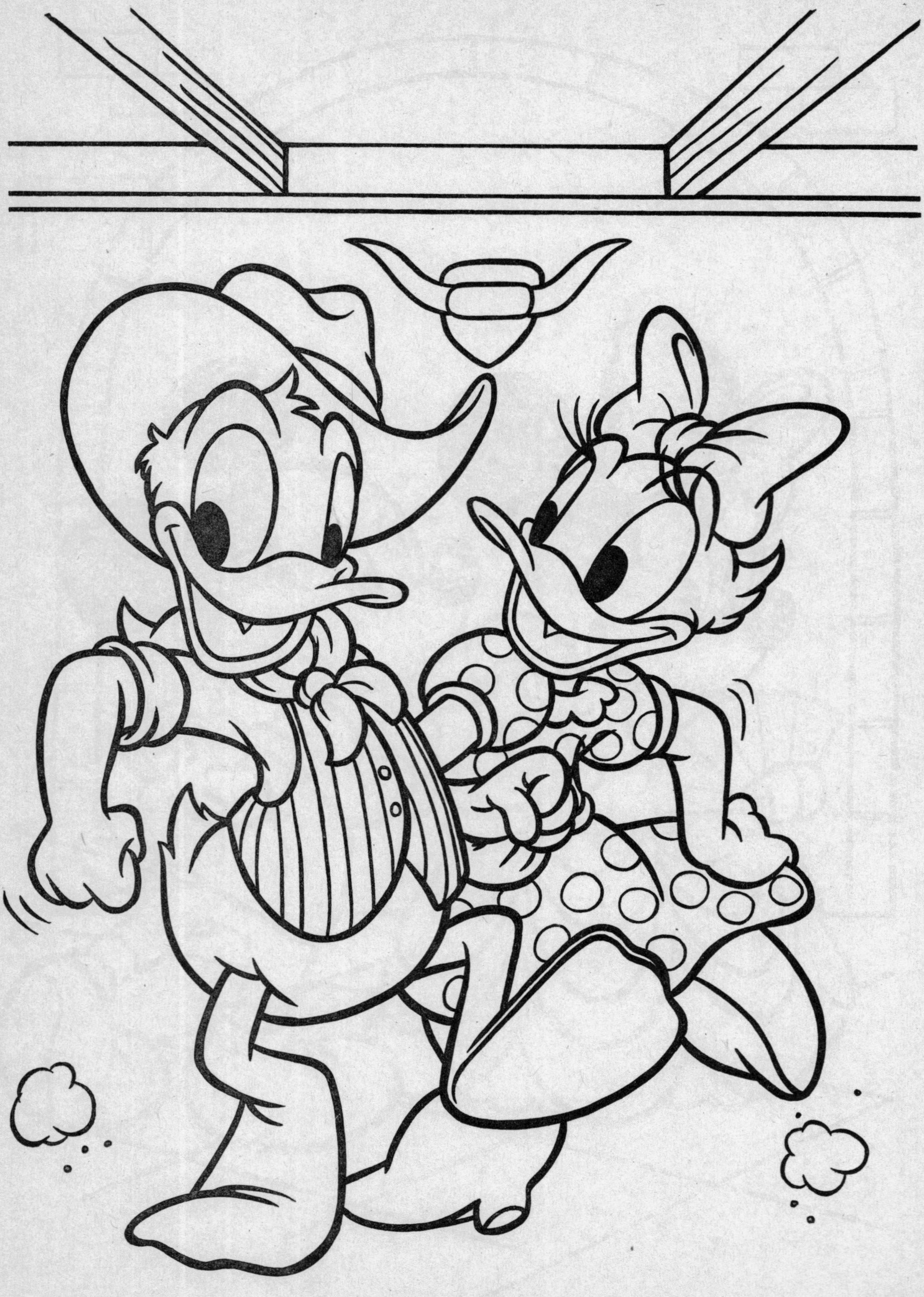

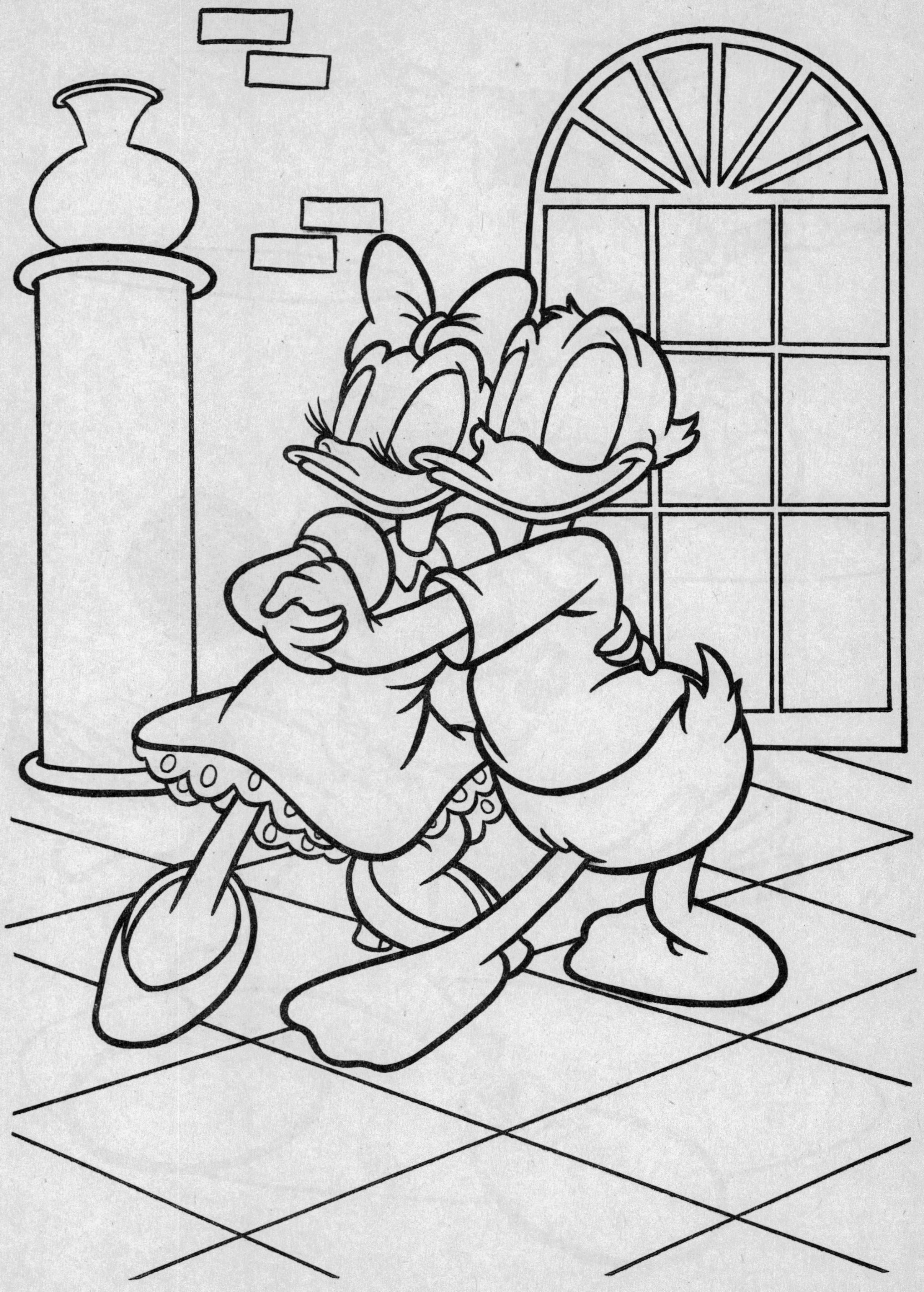

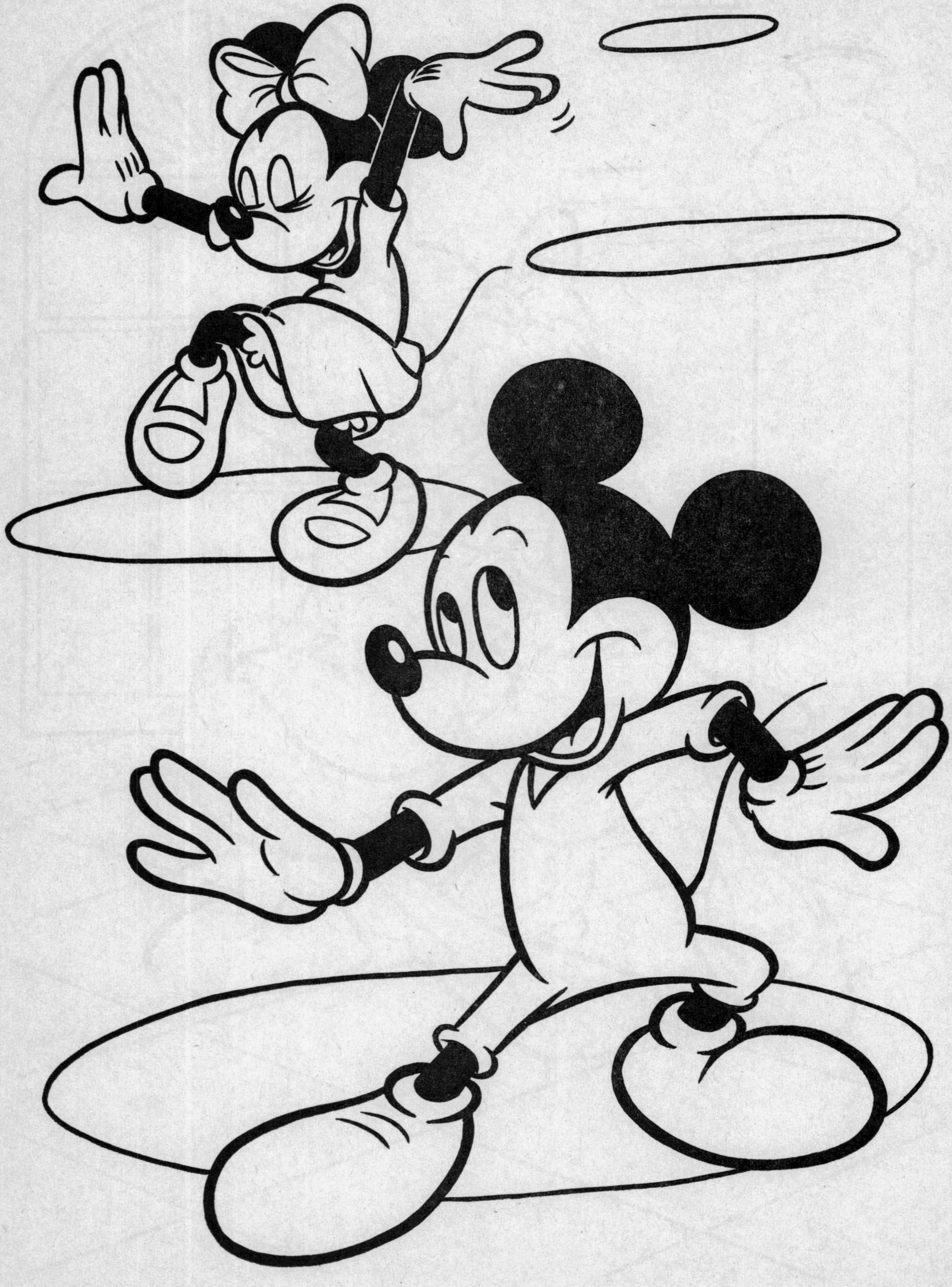

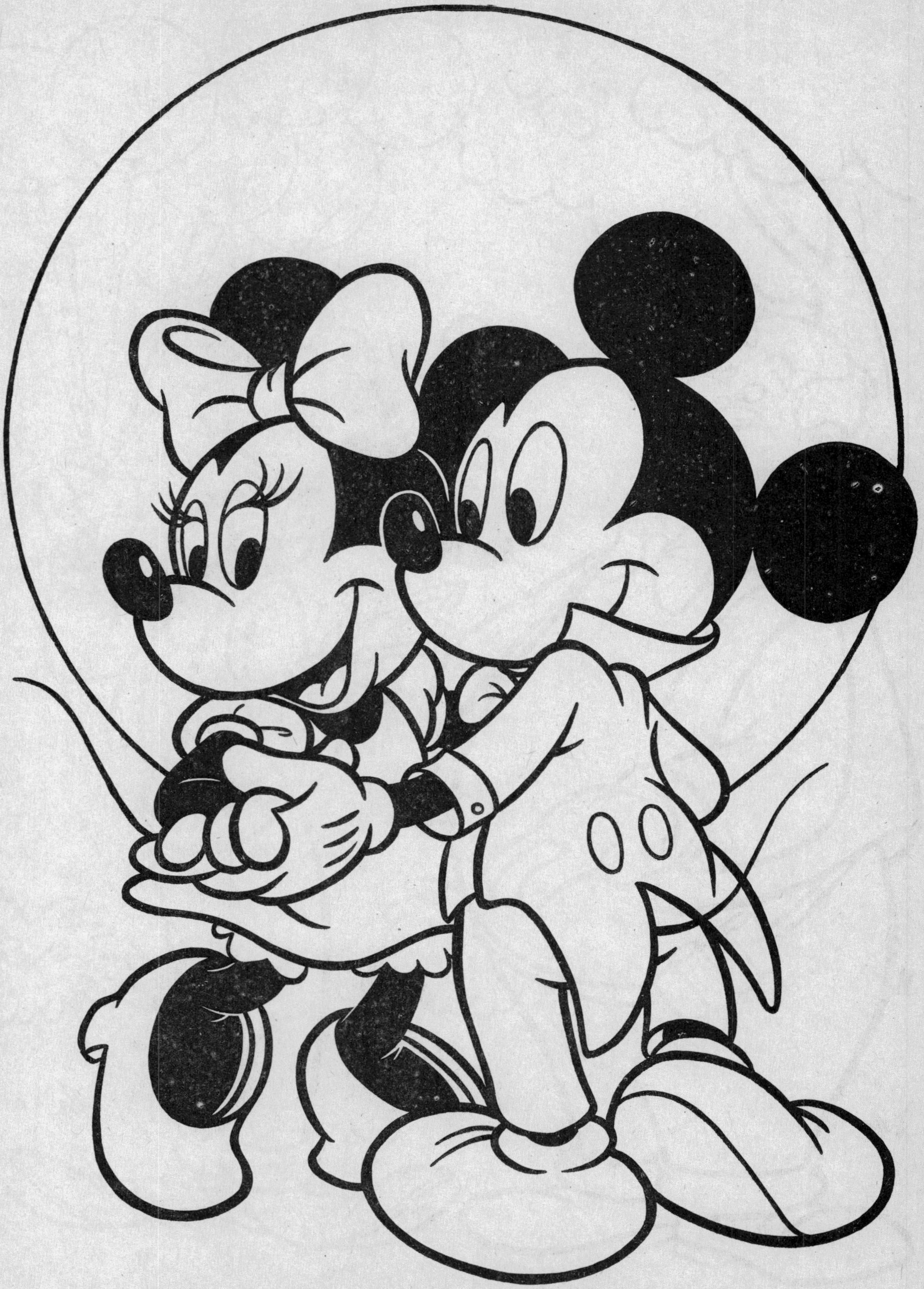

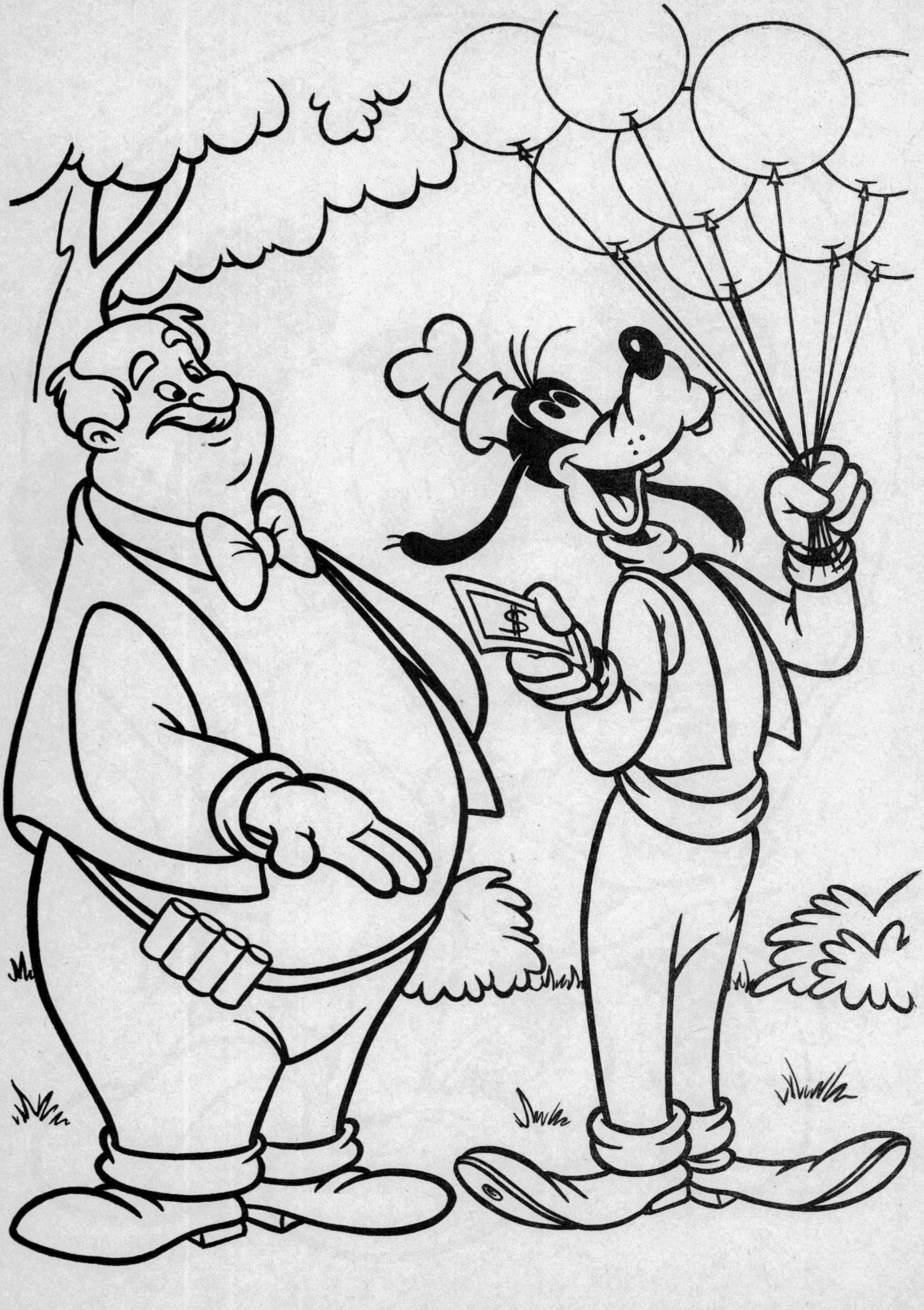

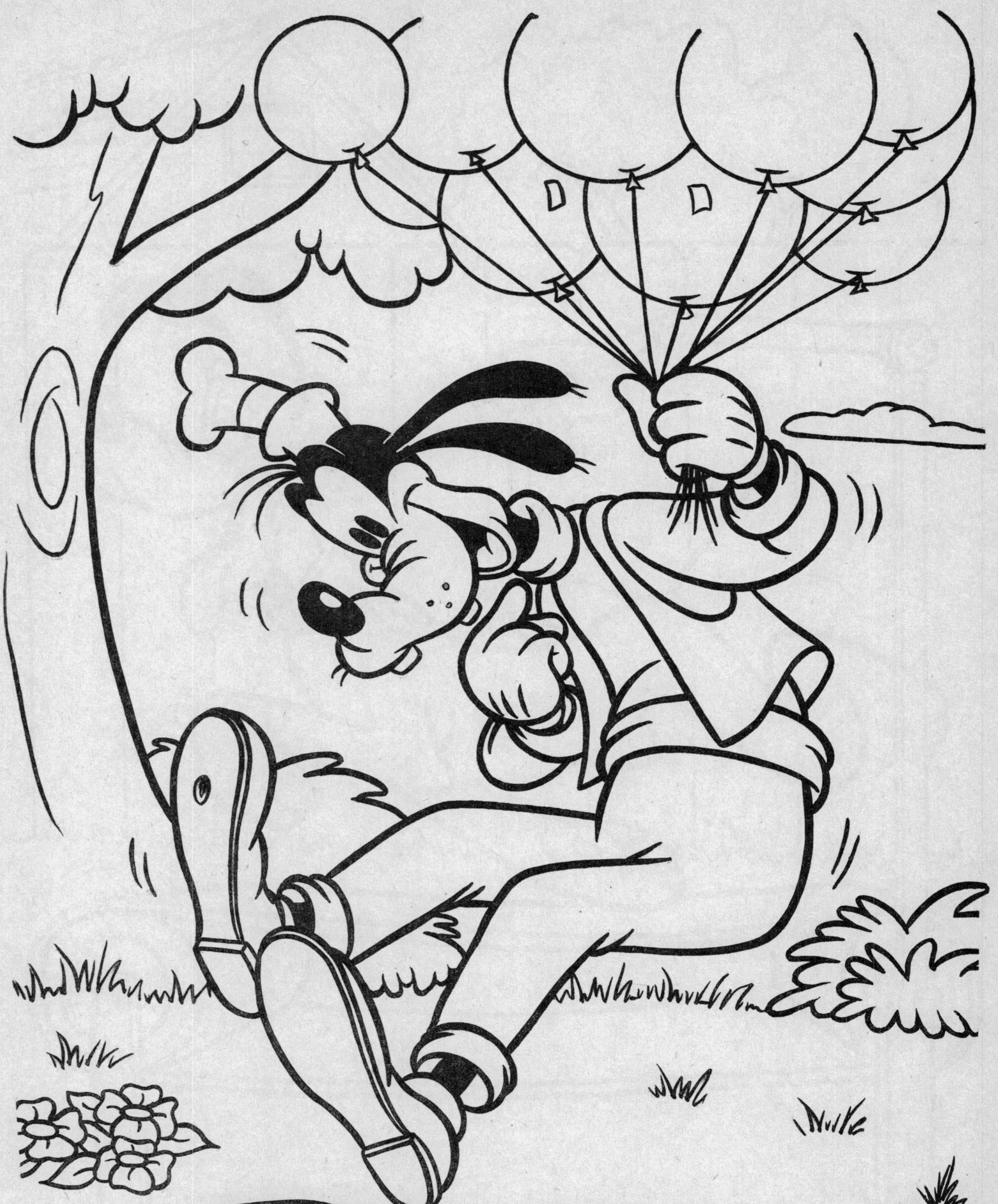

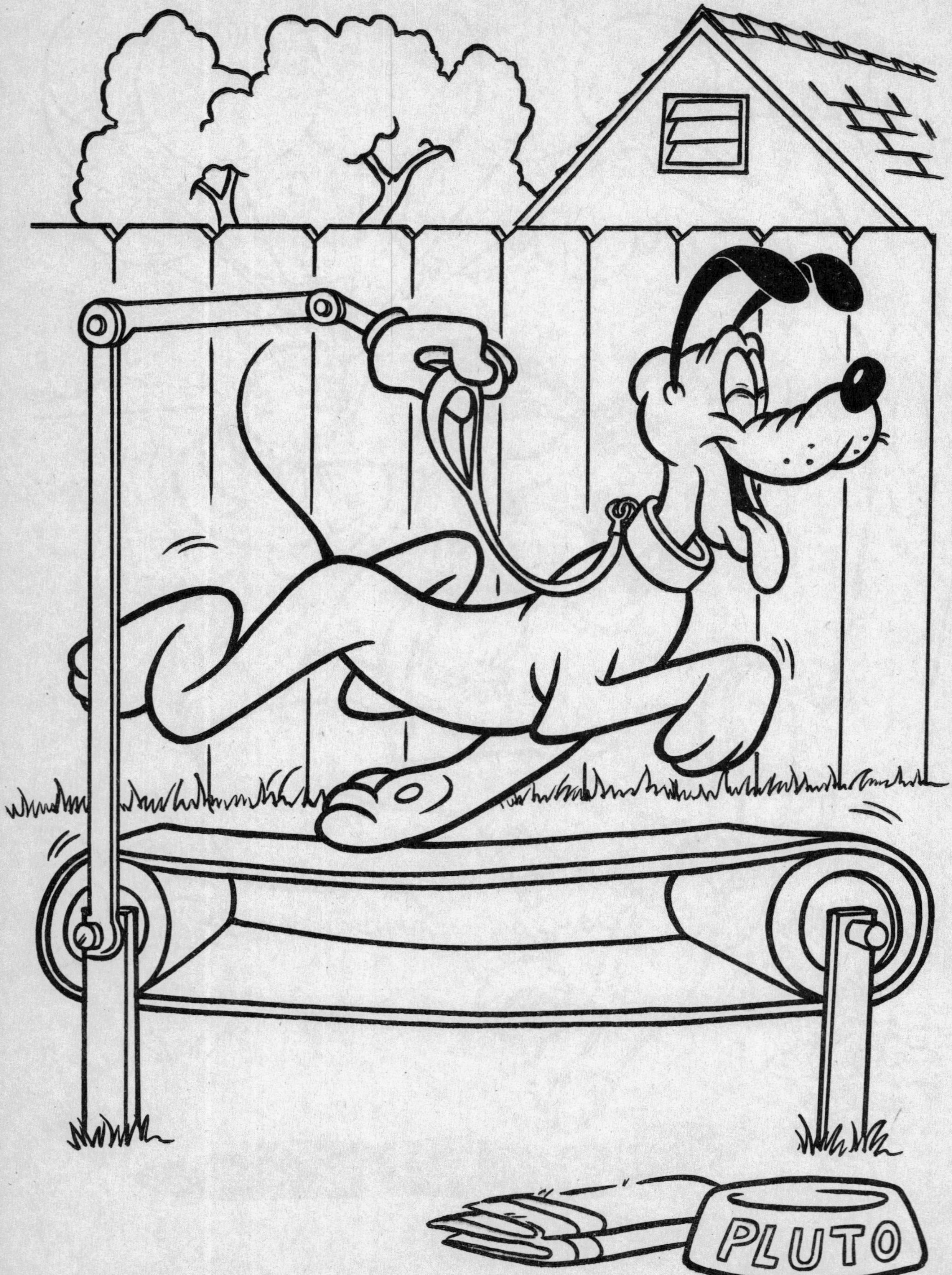
PLUTO

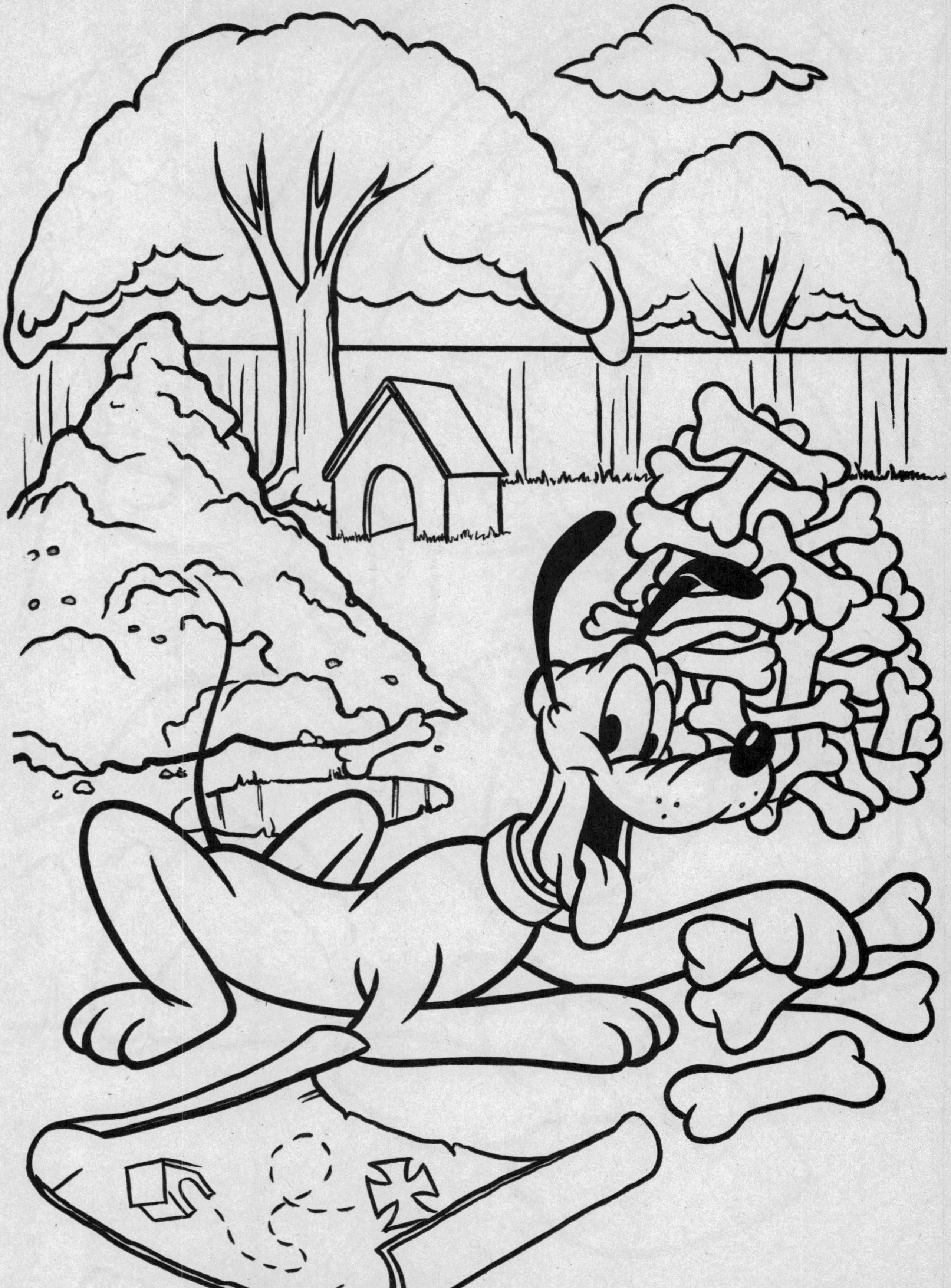

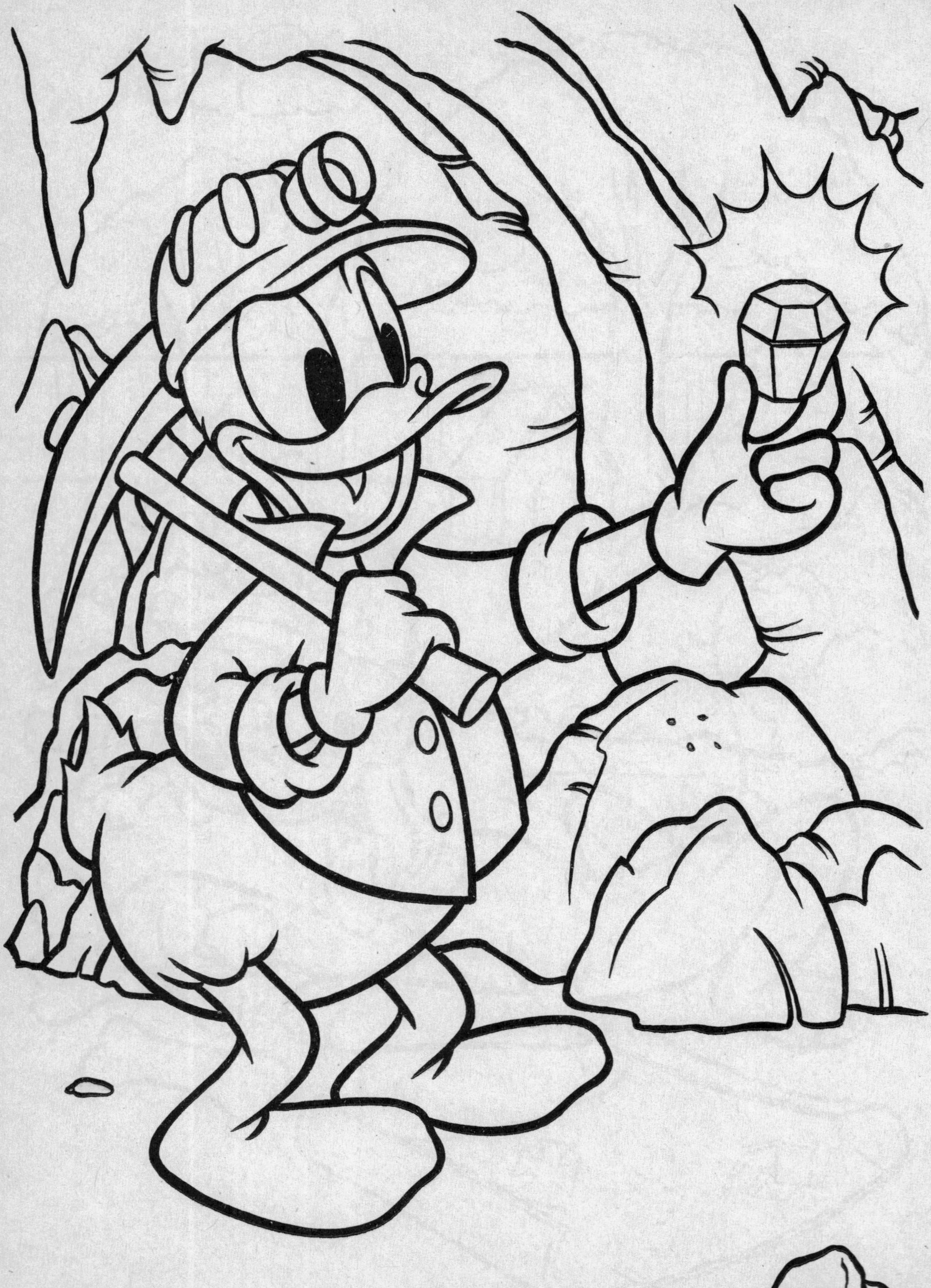

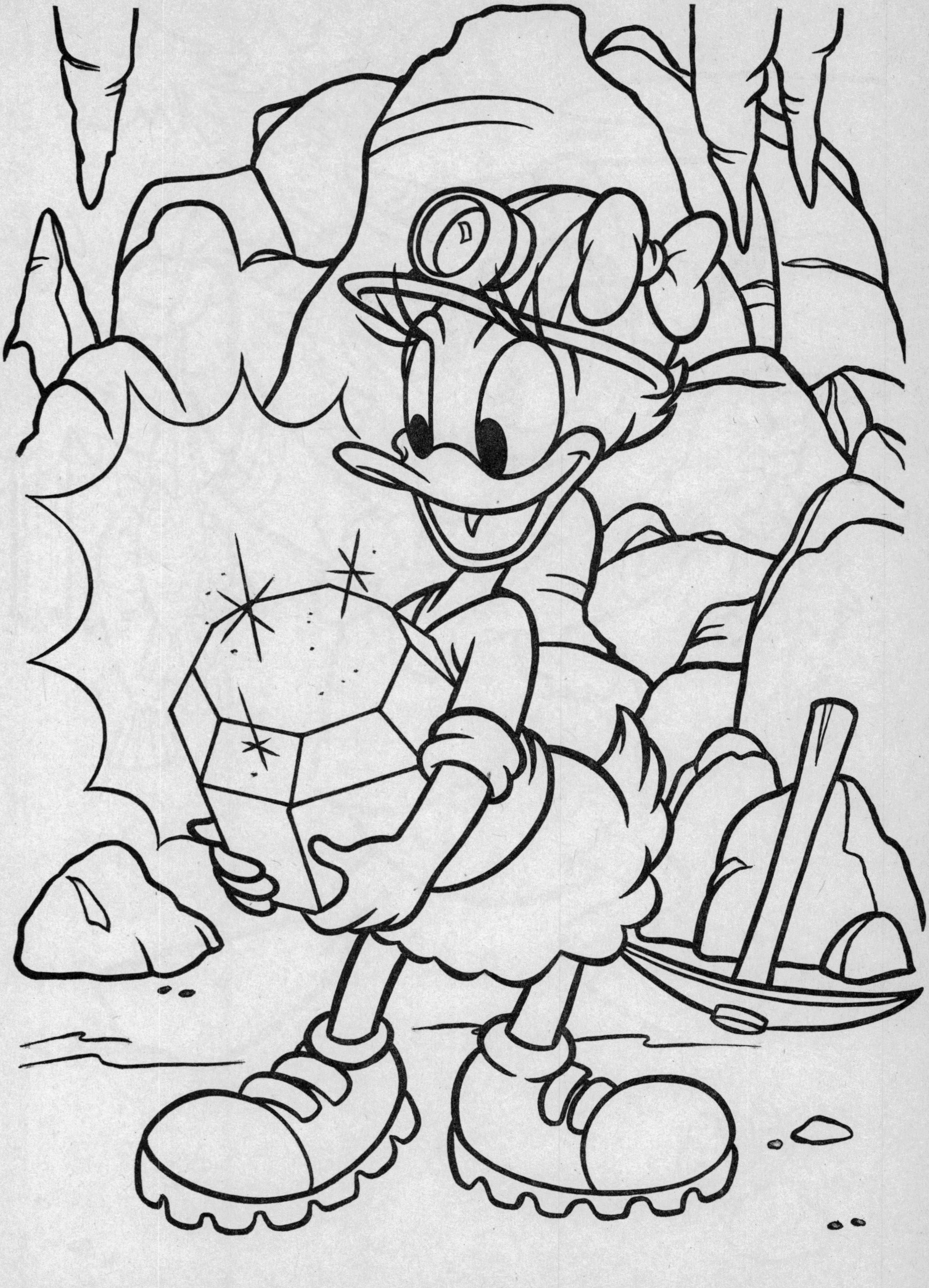

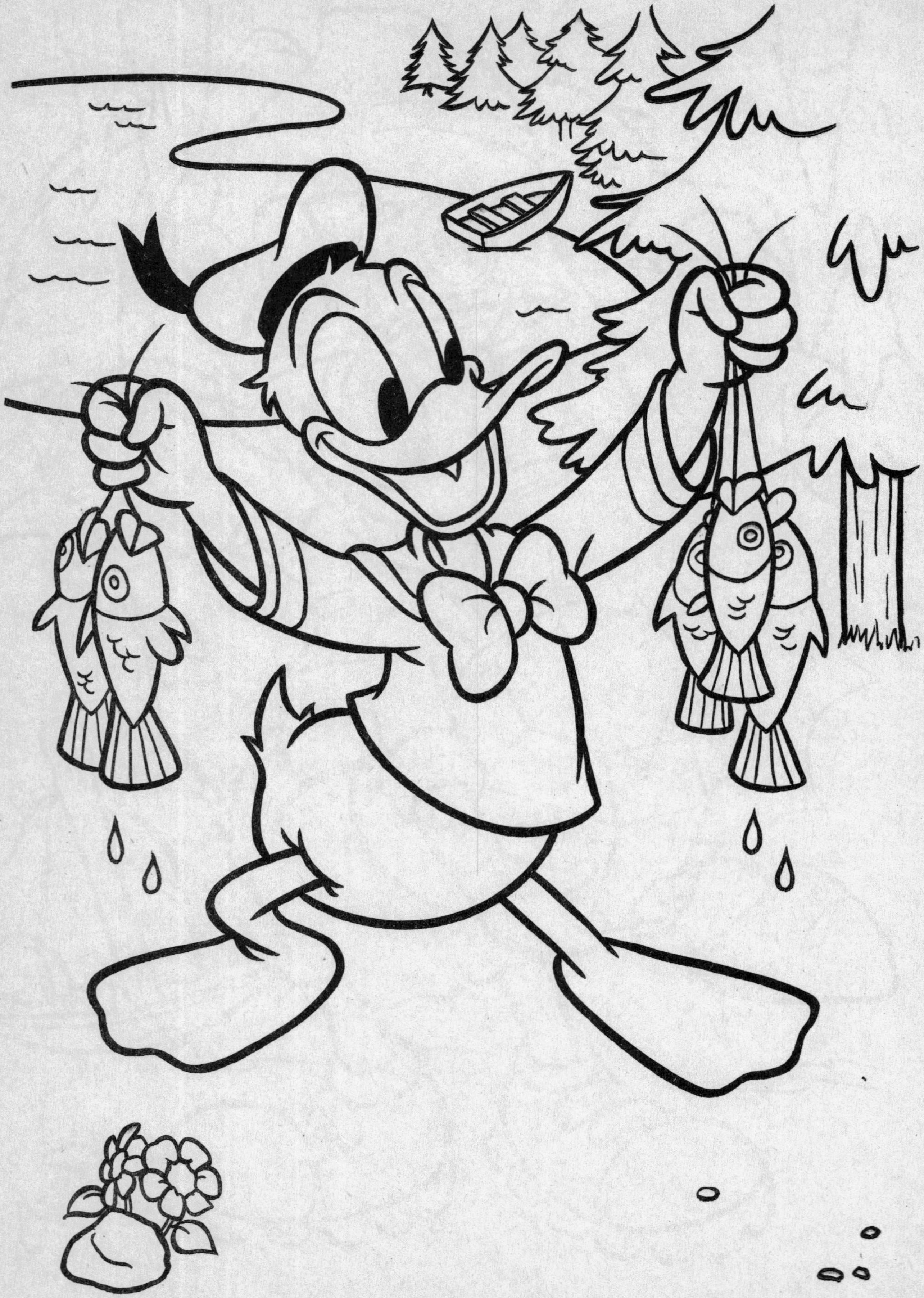

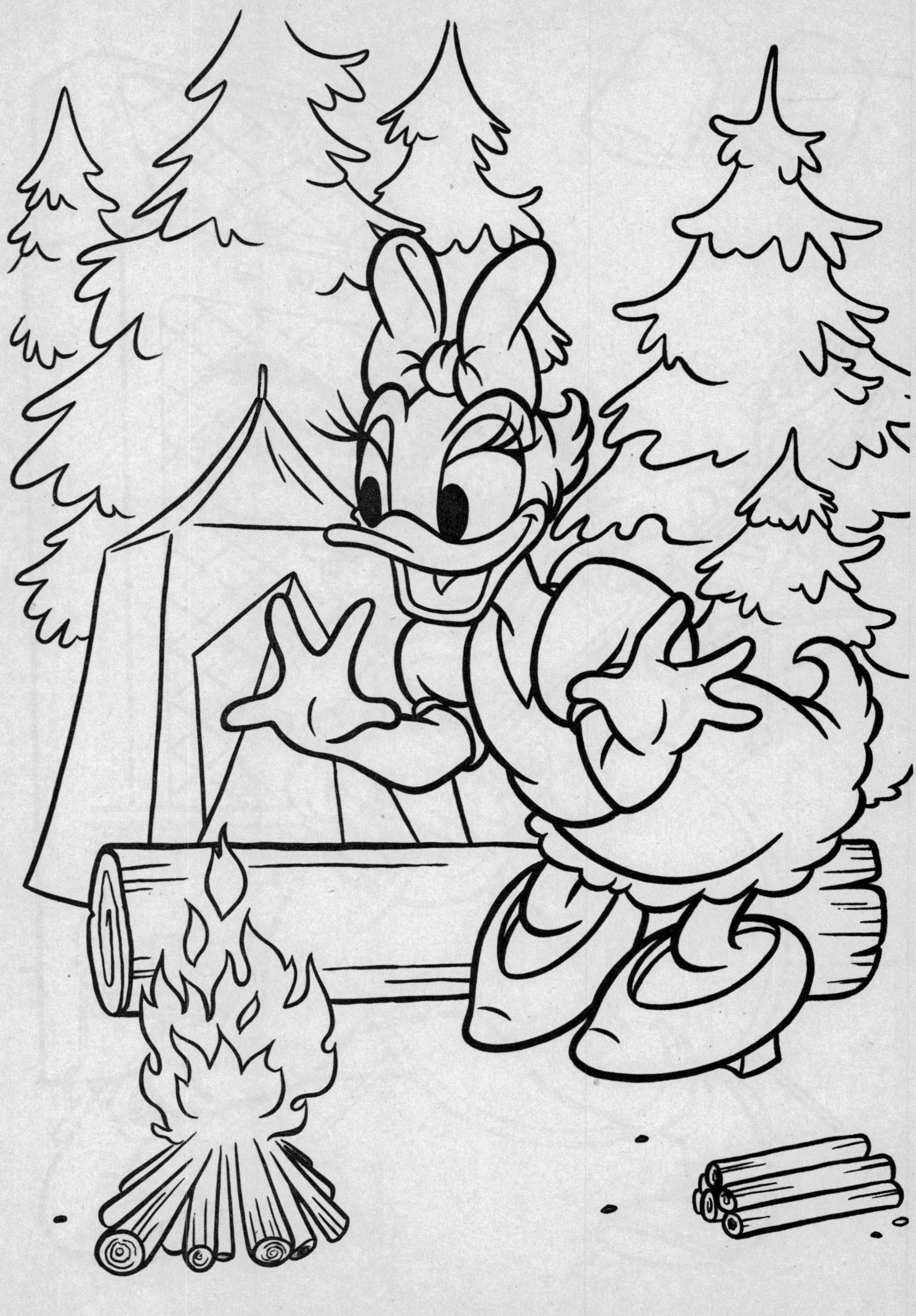

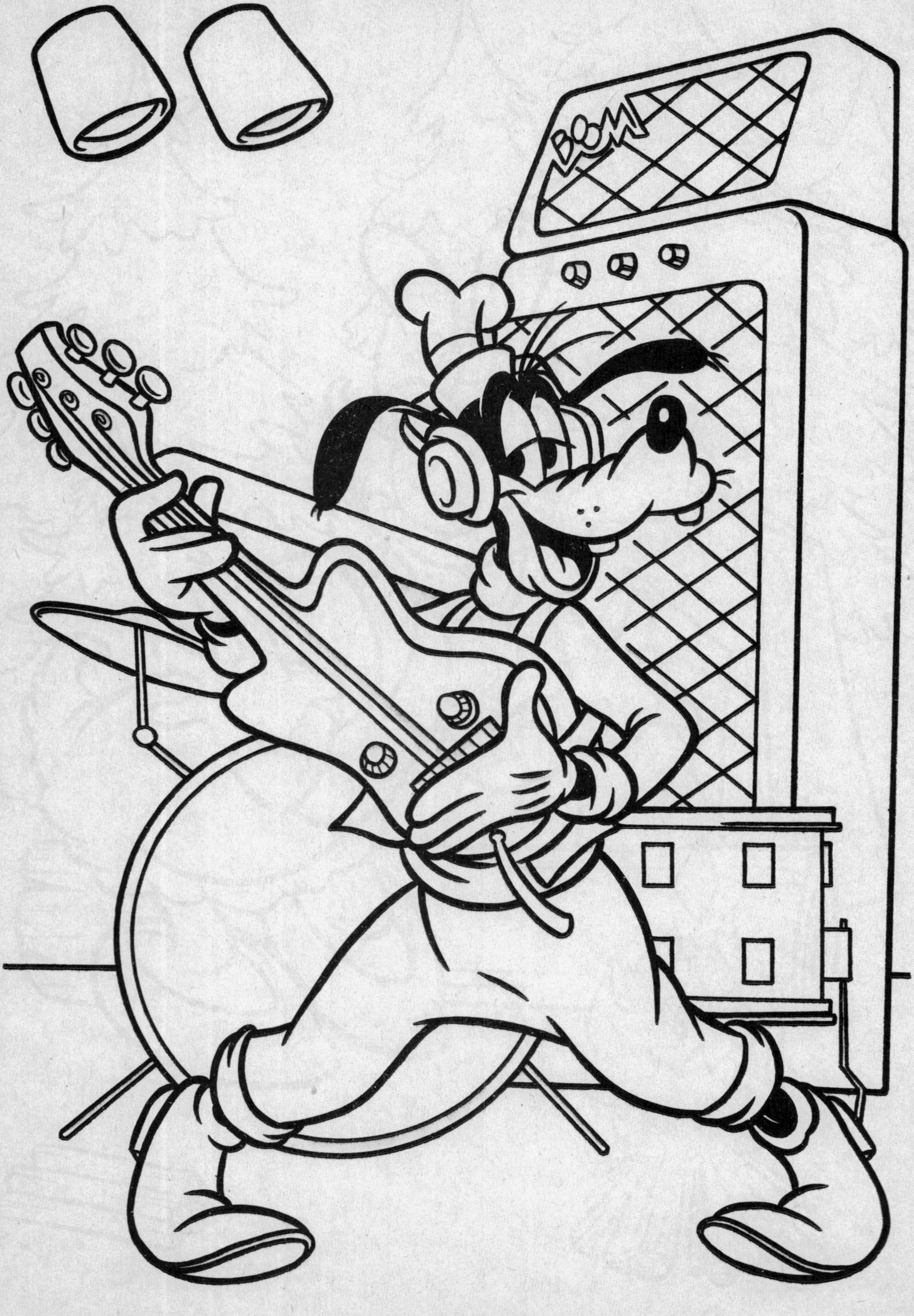
BOOM

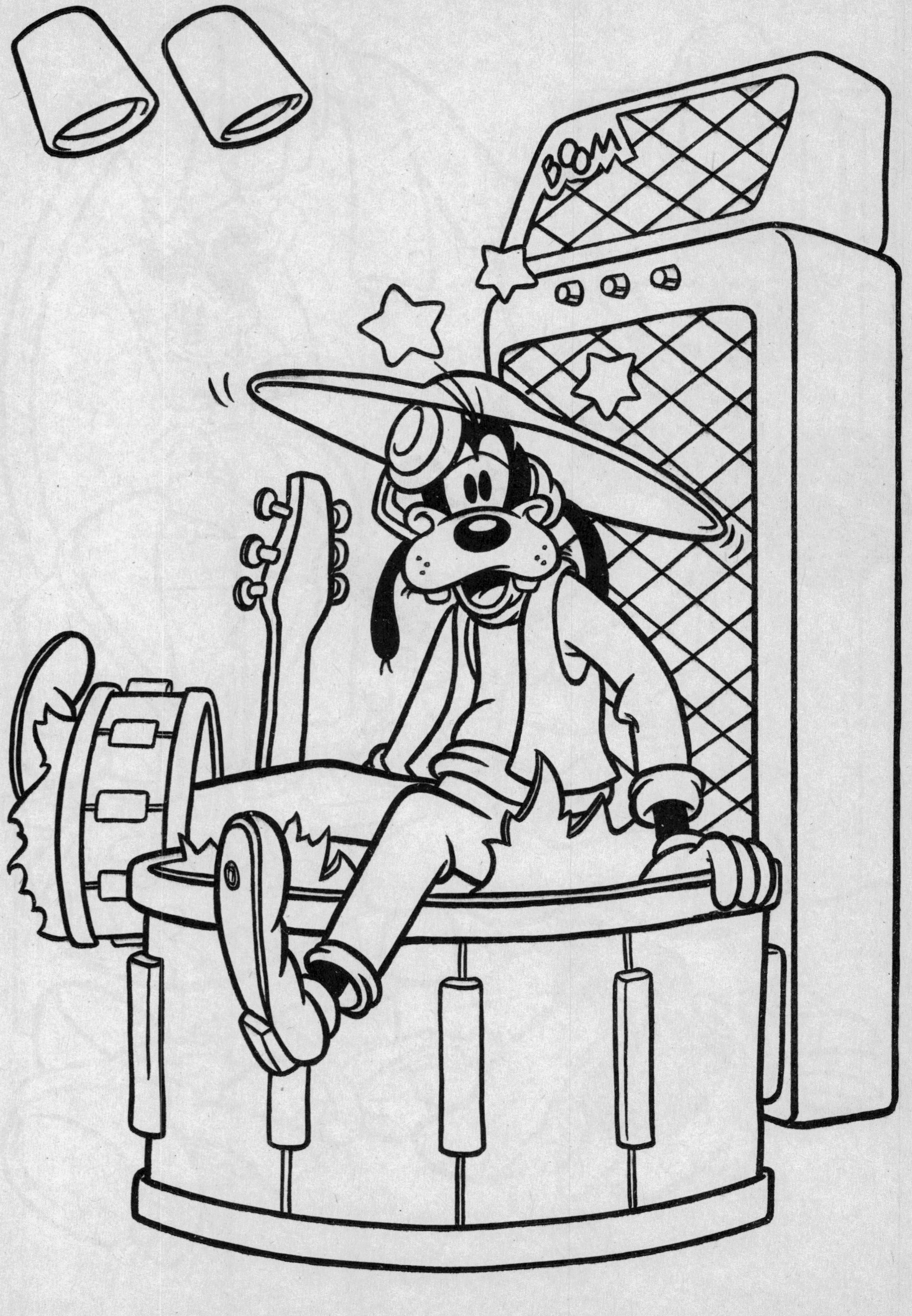
BOOM

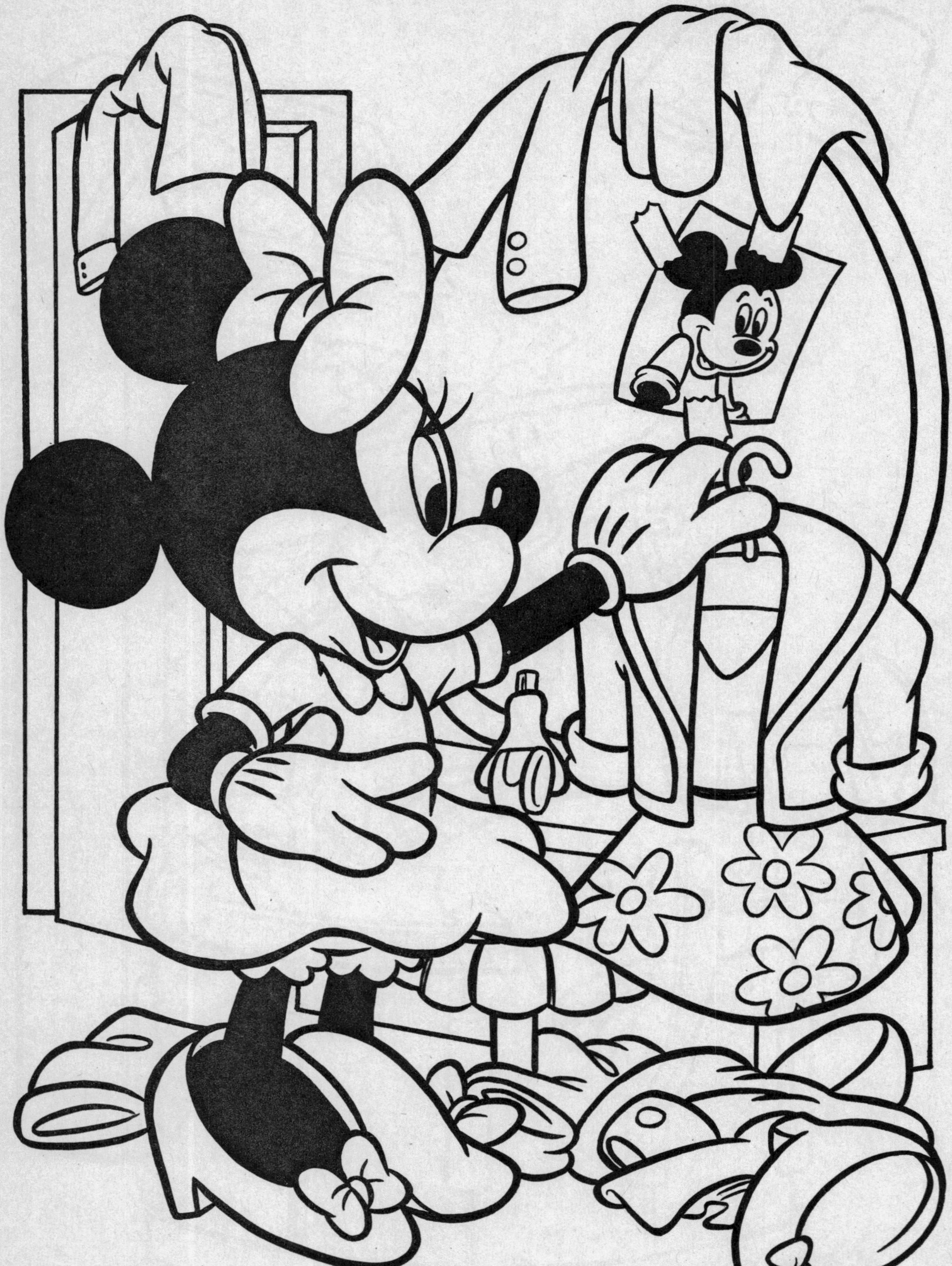

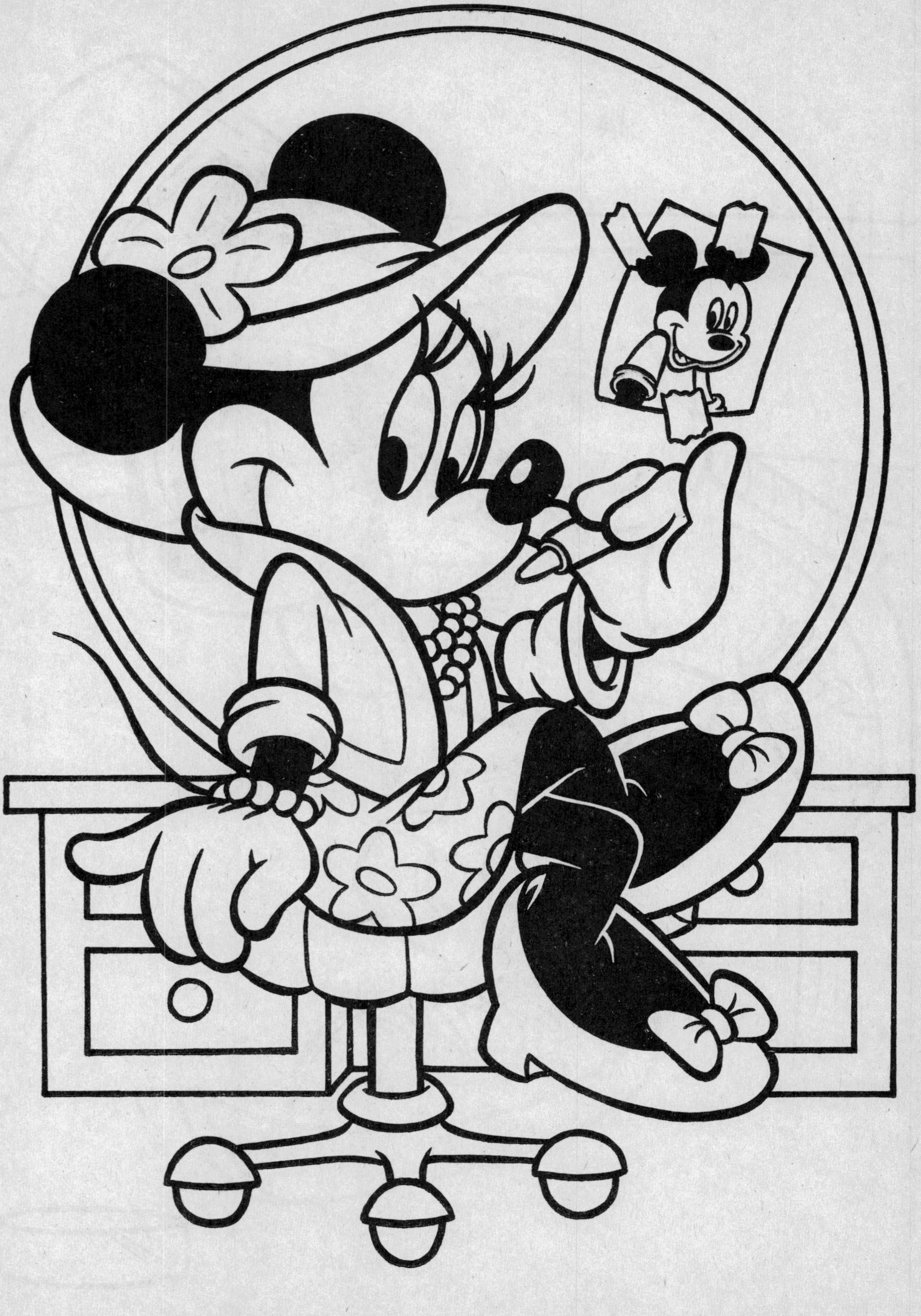

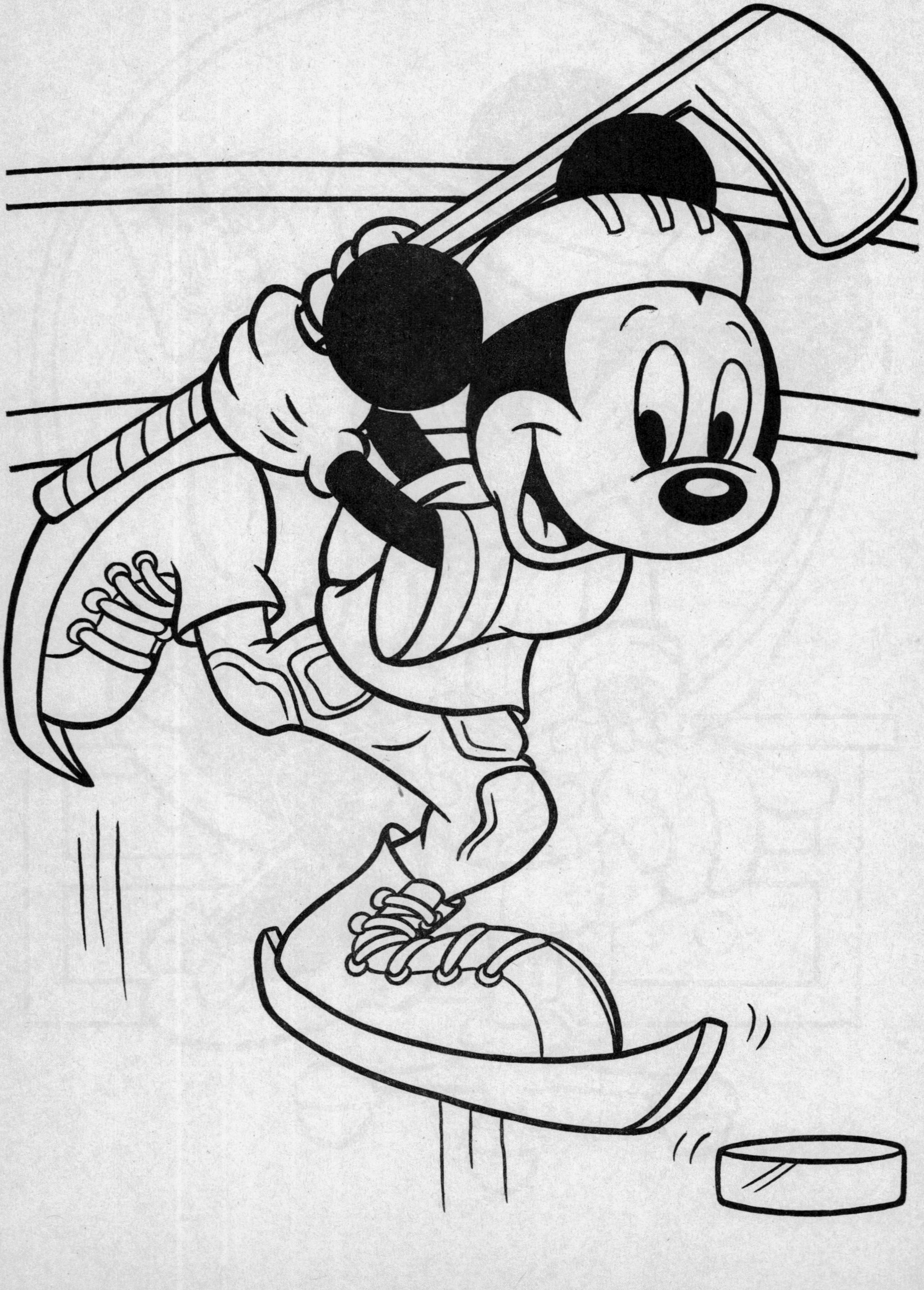

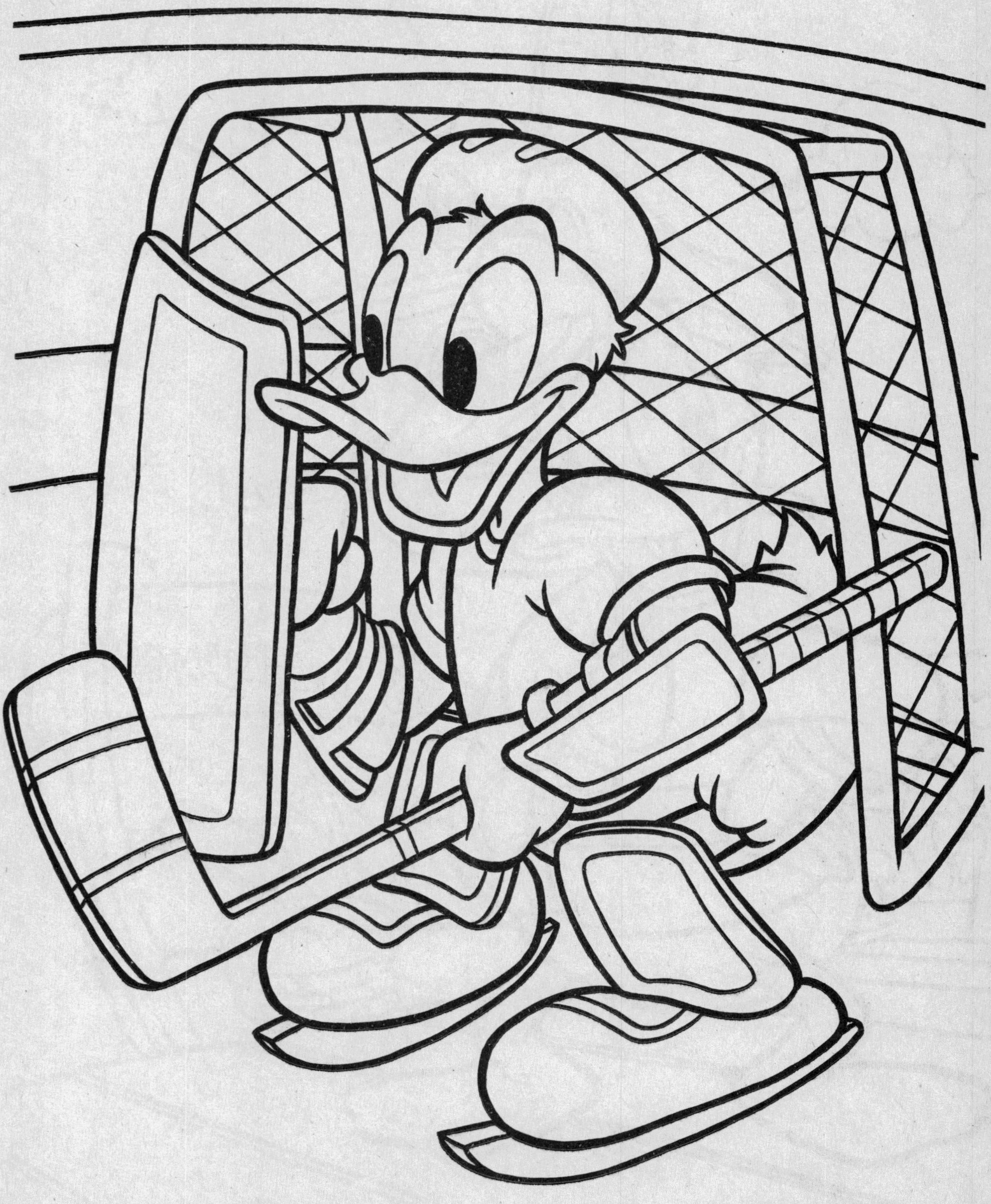

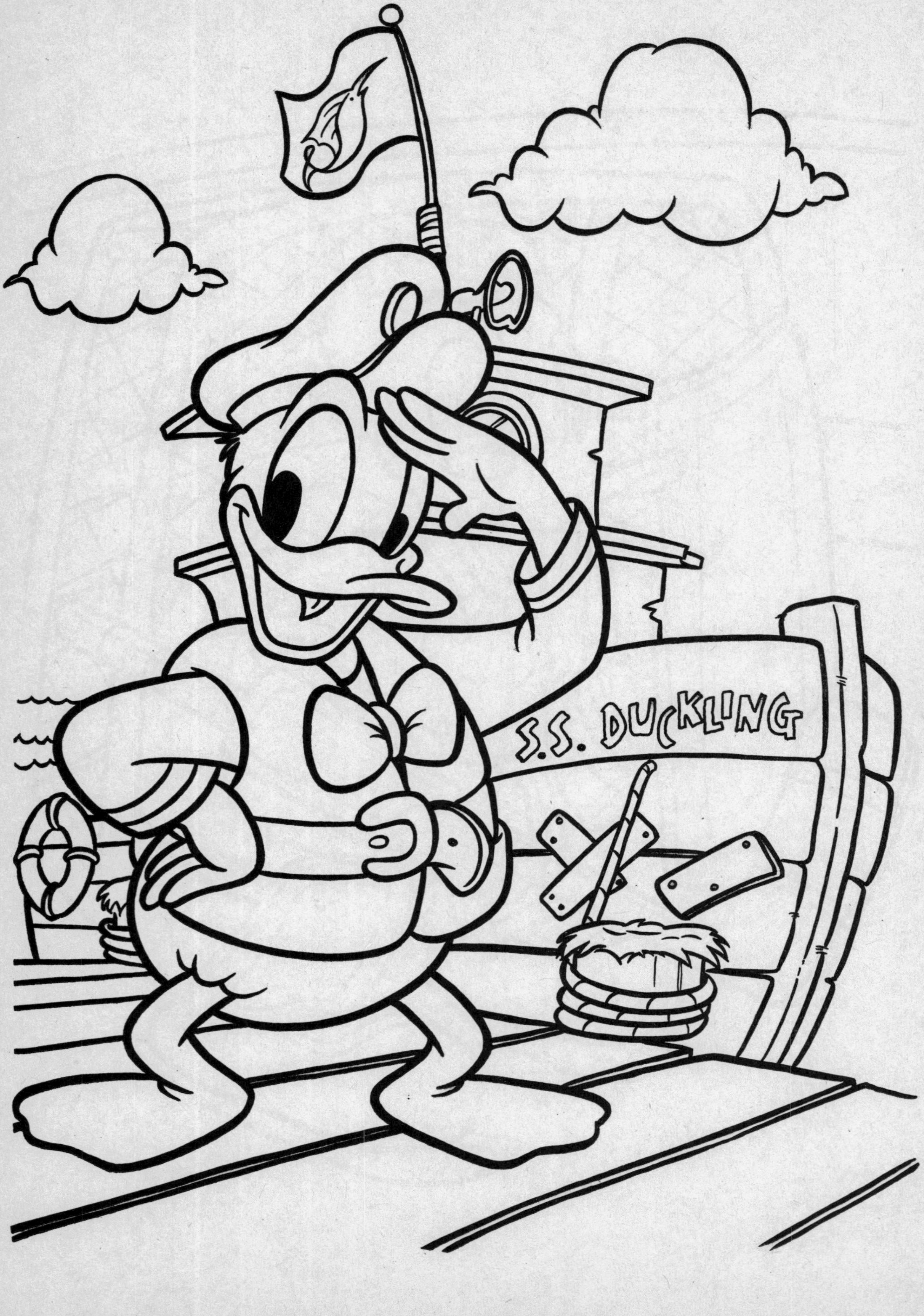
S.S. DUCKLING

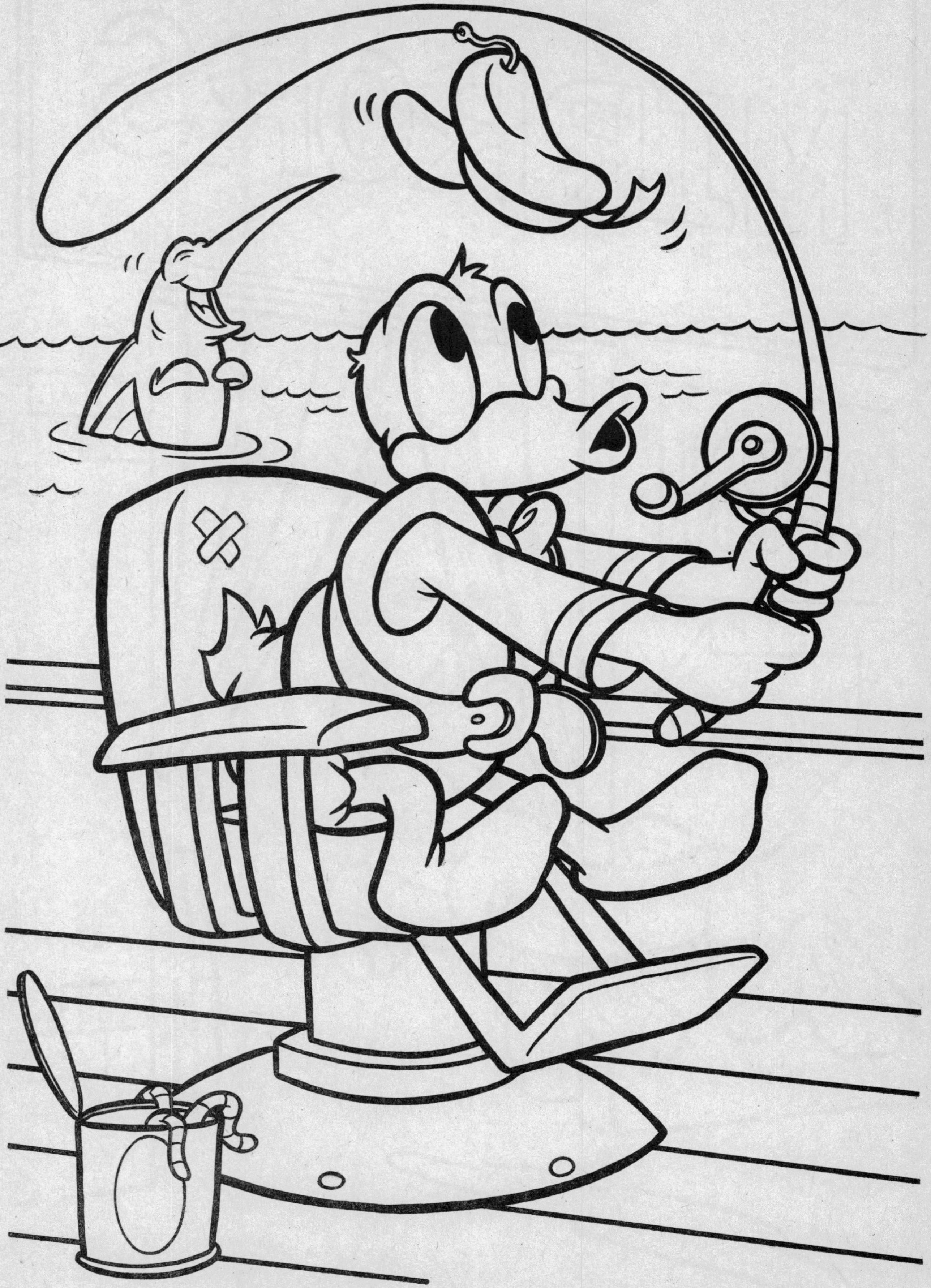

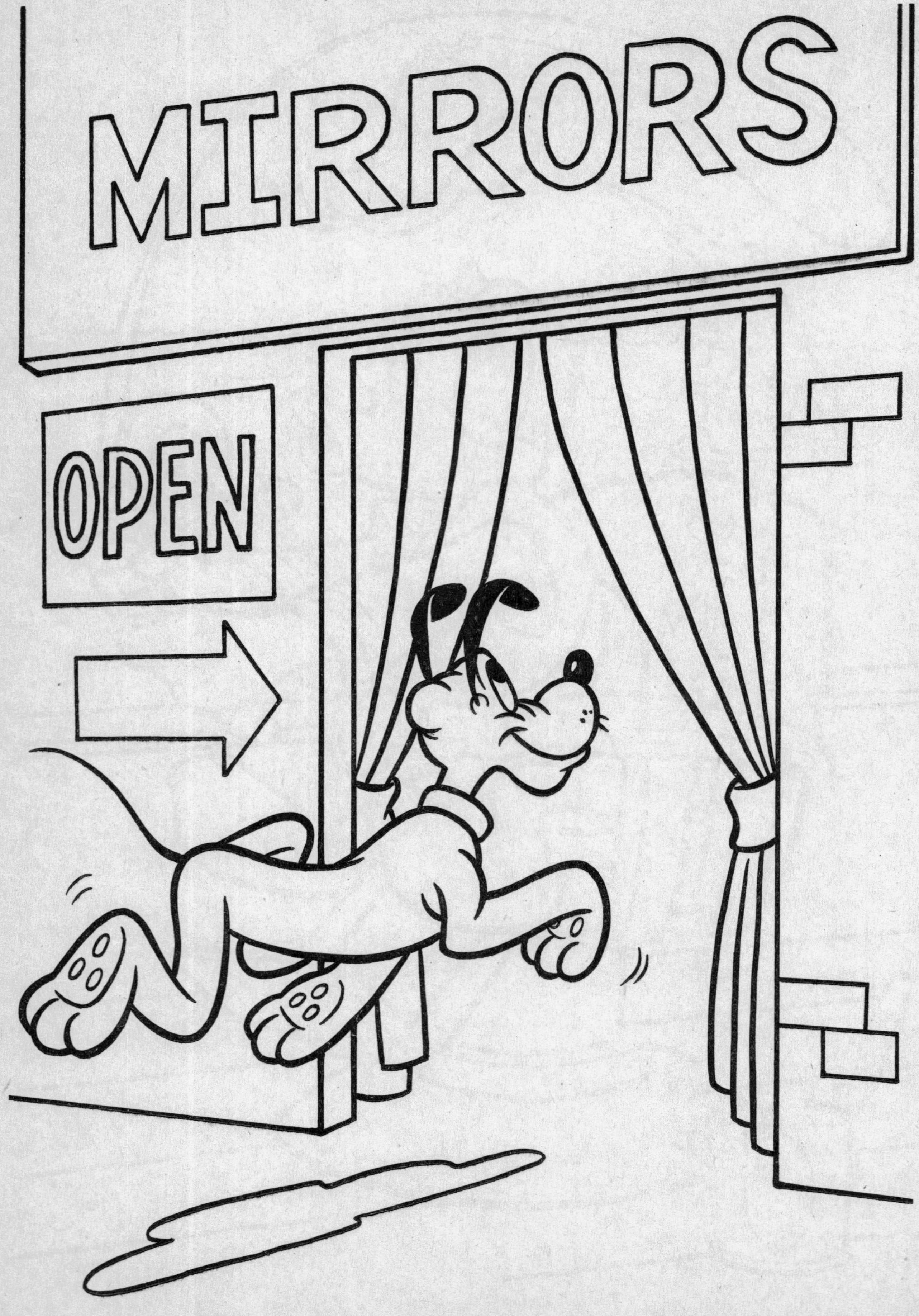
MIRRORS
OPEN

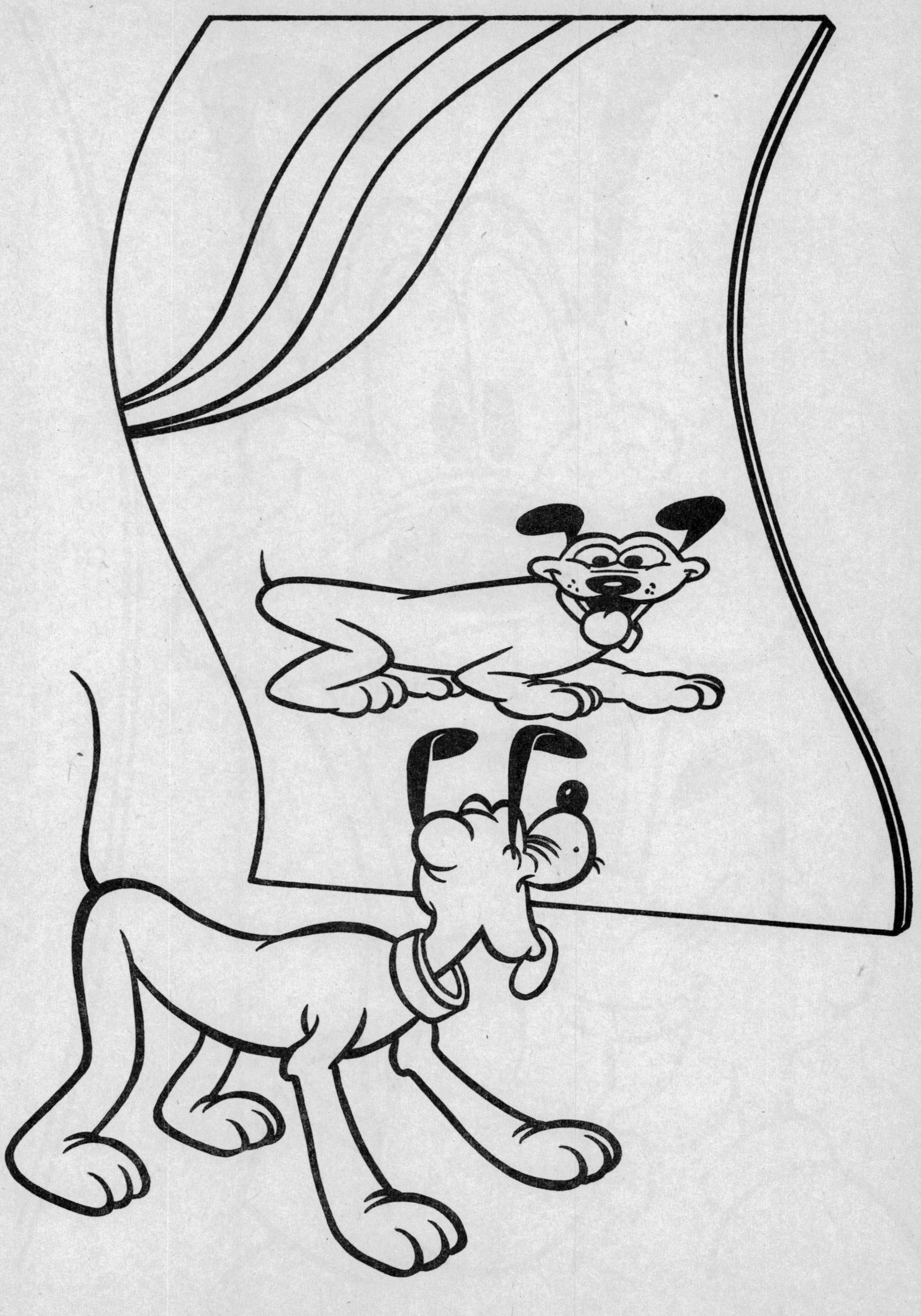

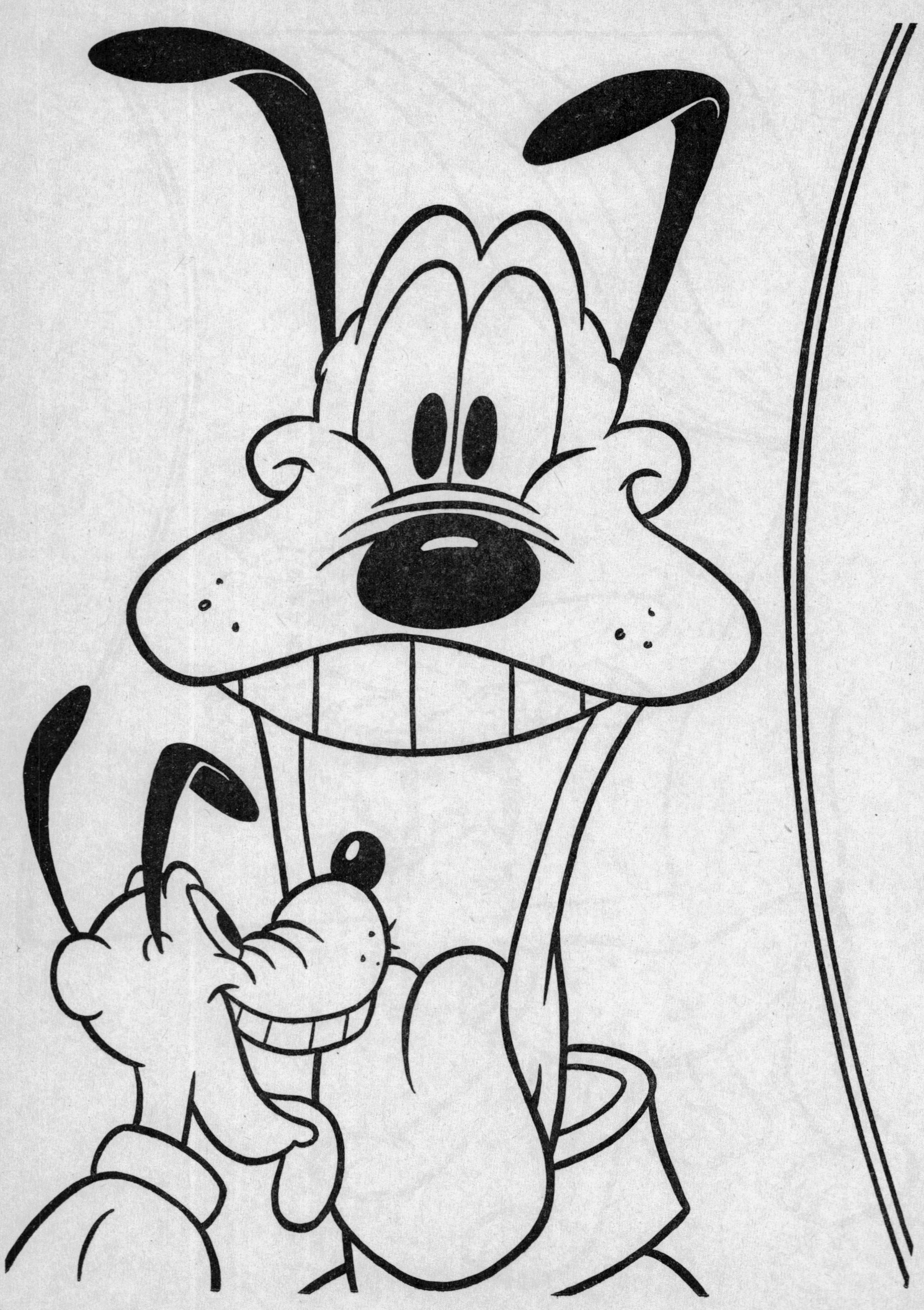

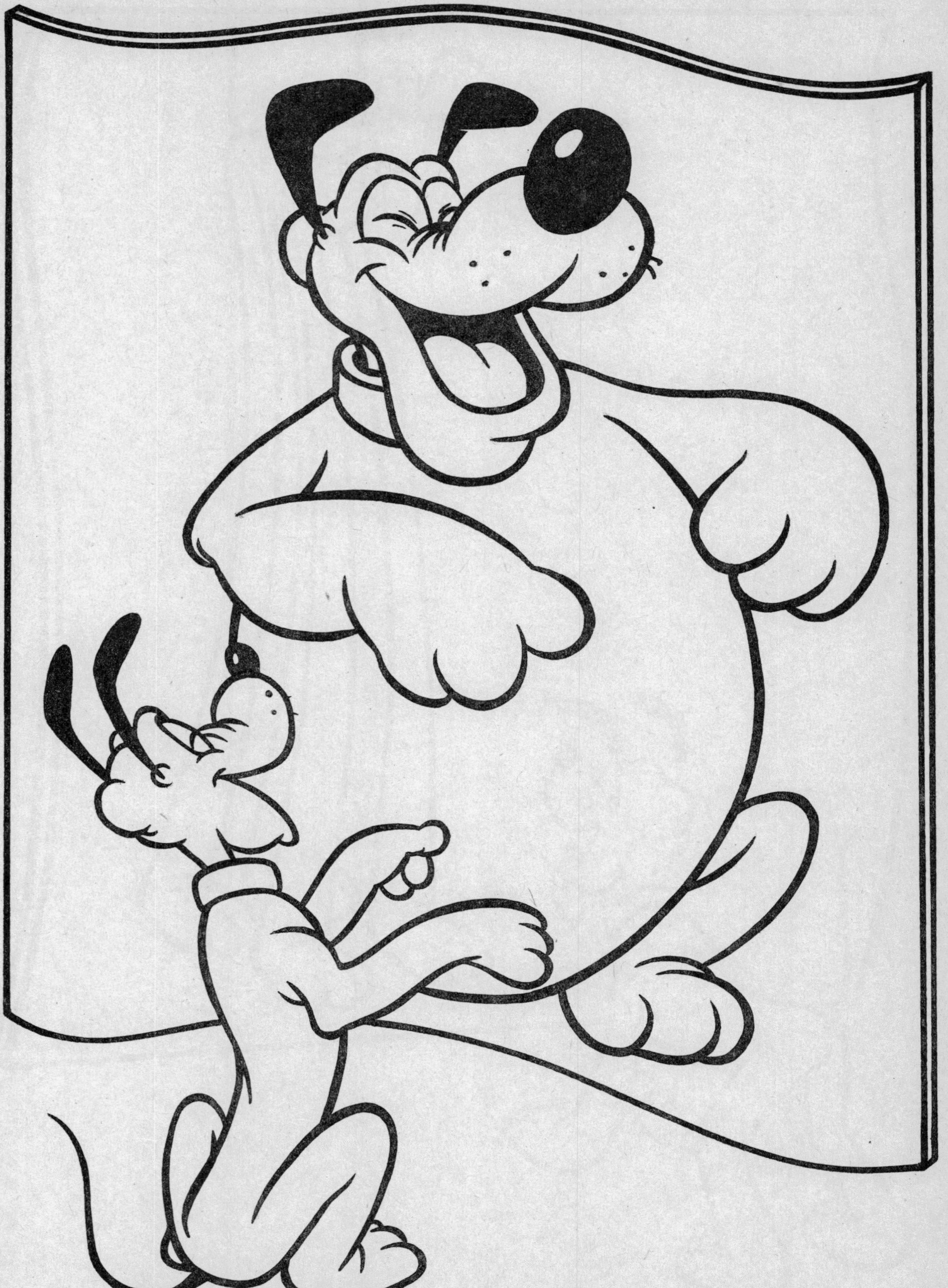

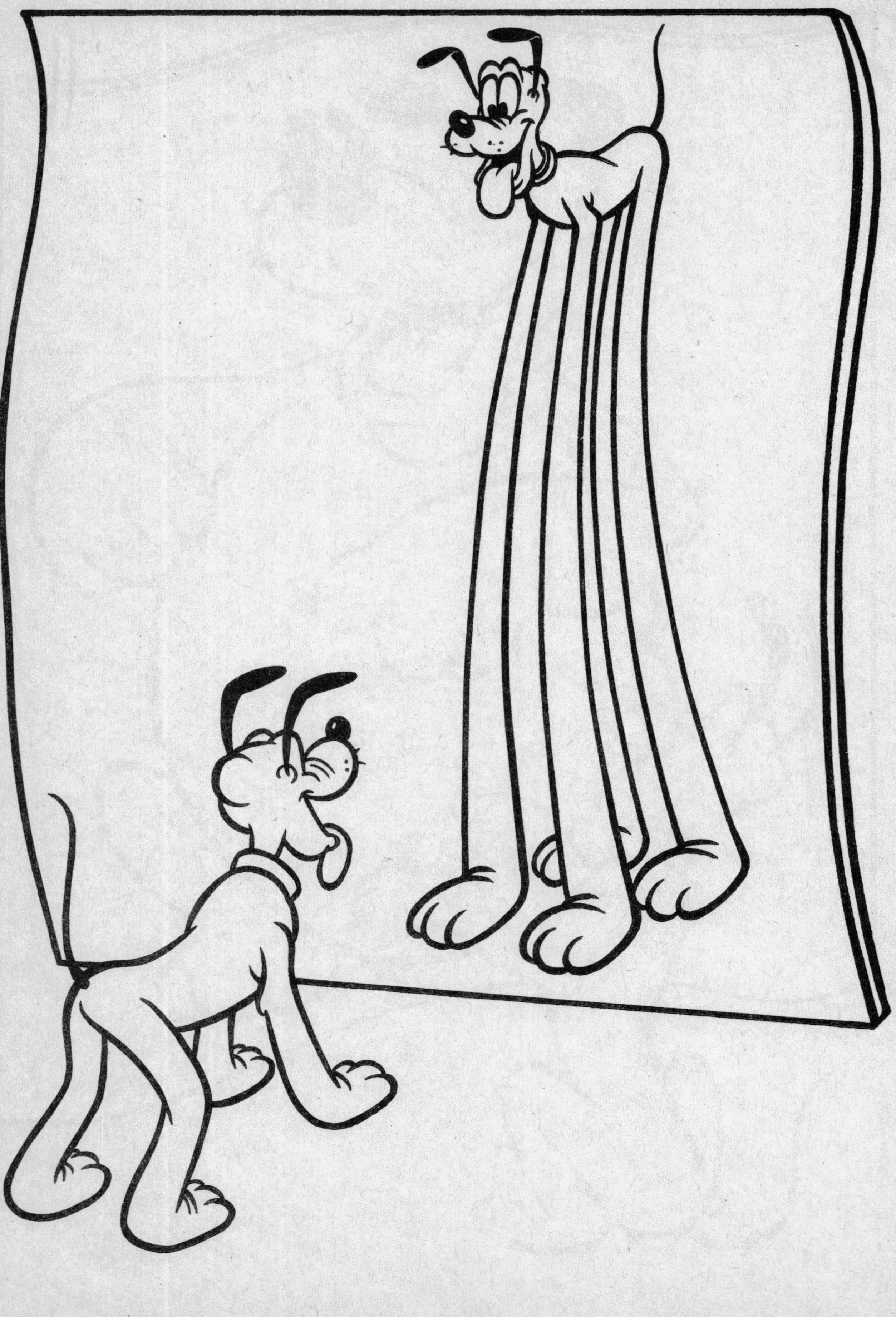

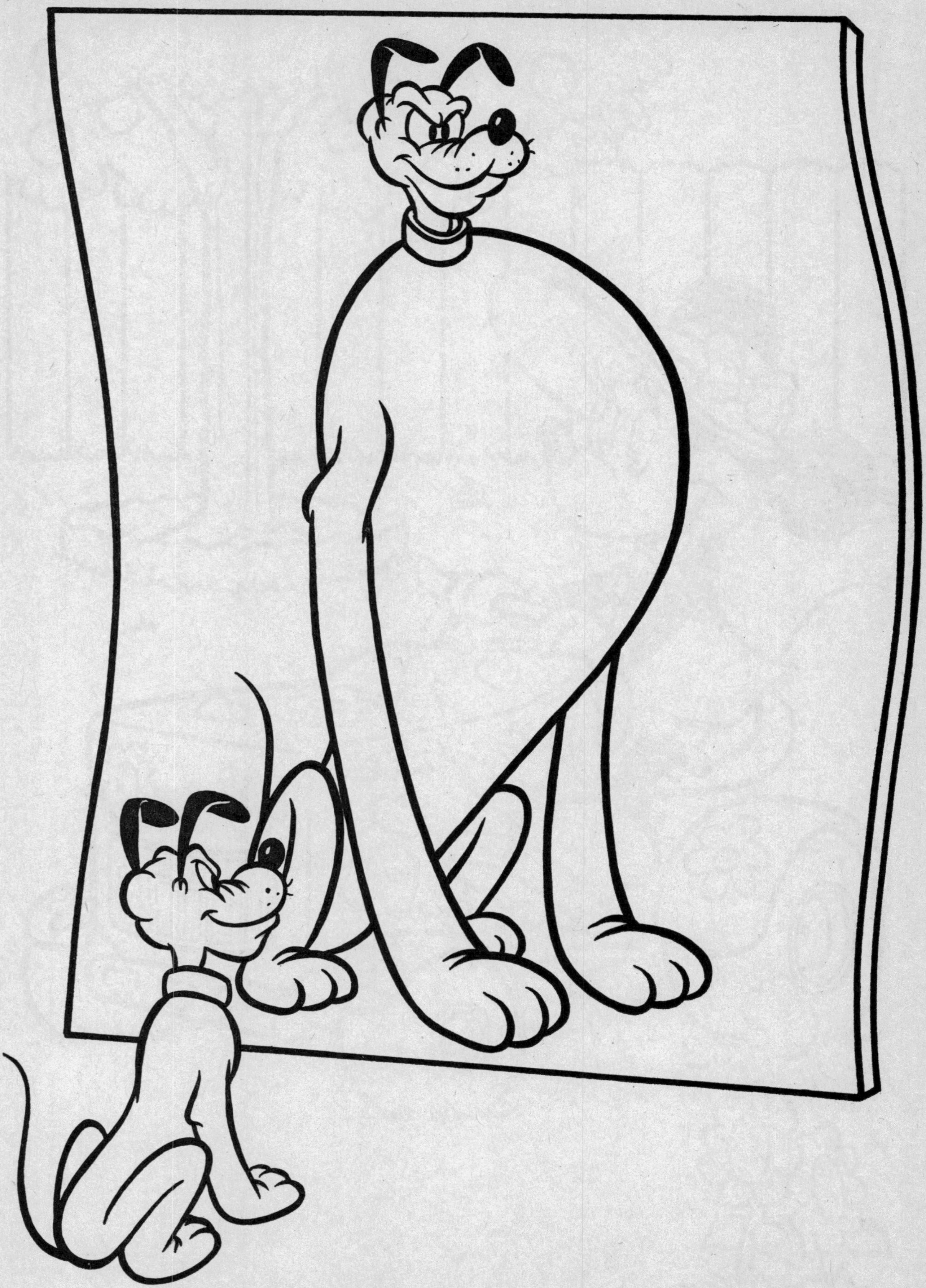

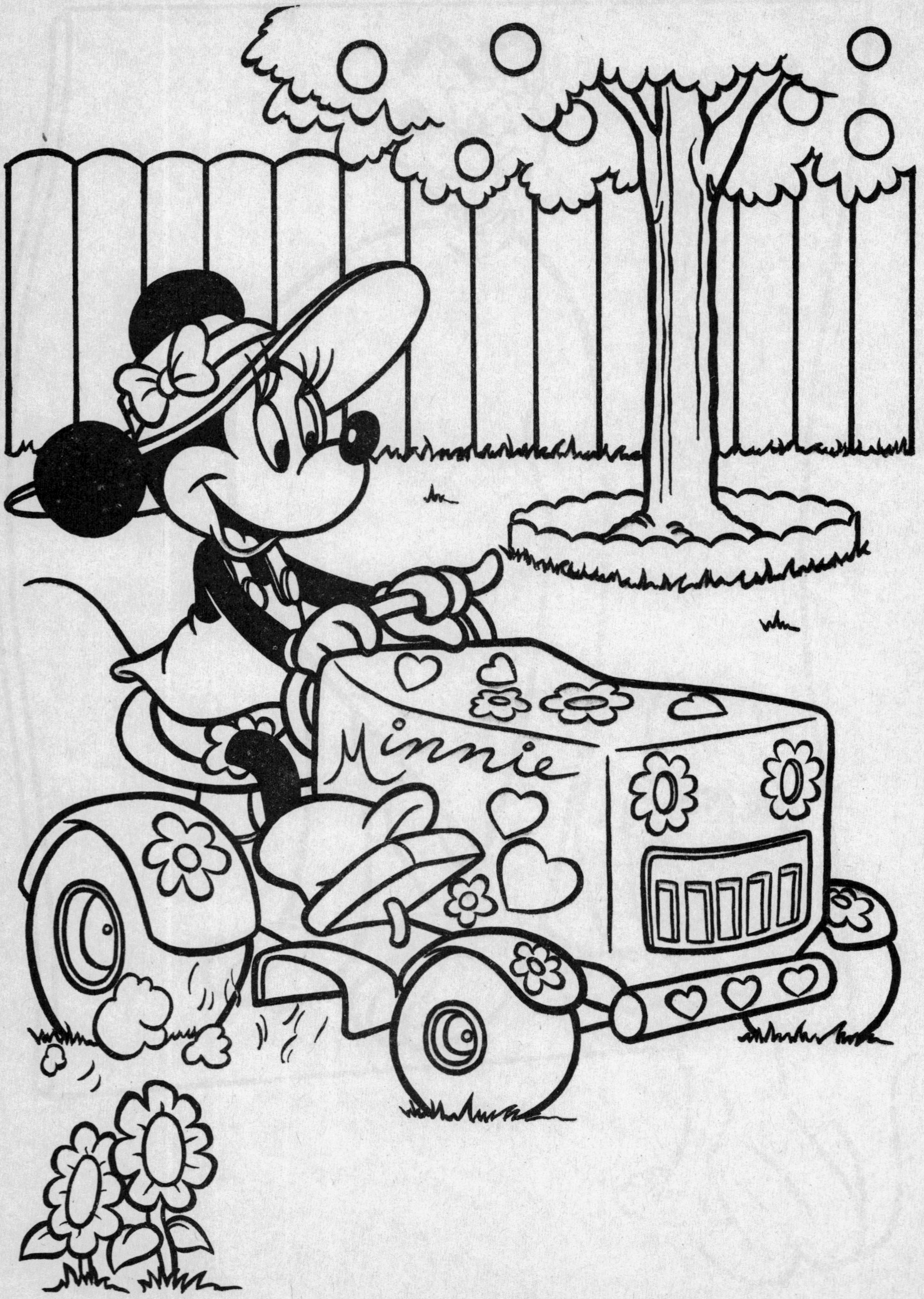
Minnie

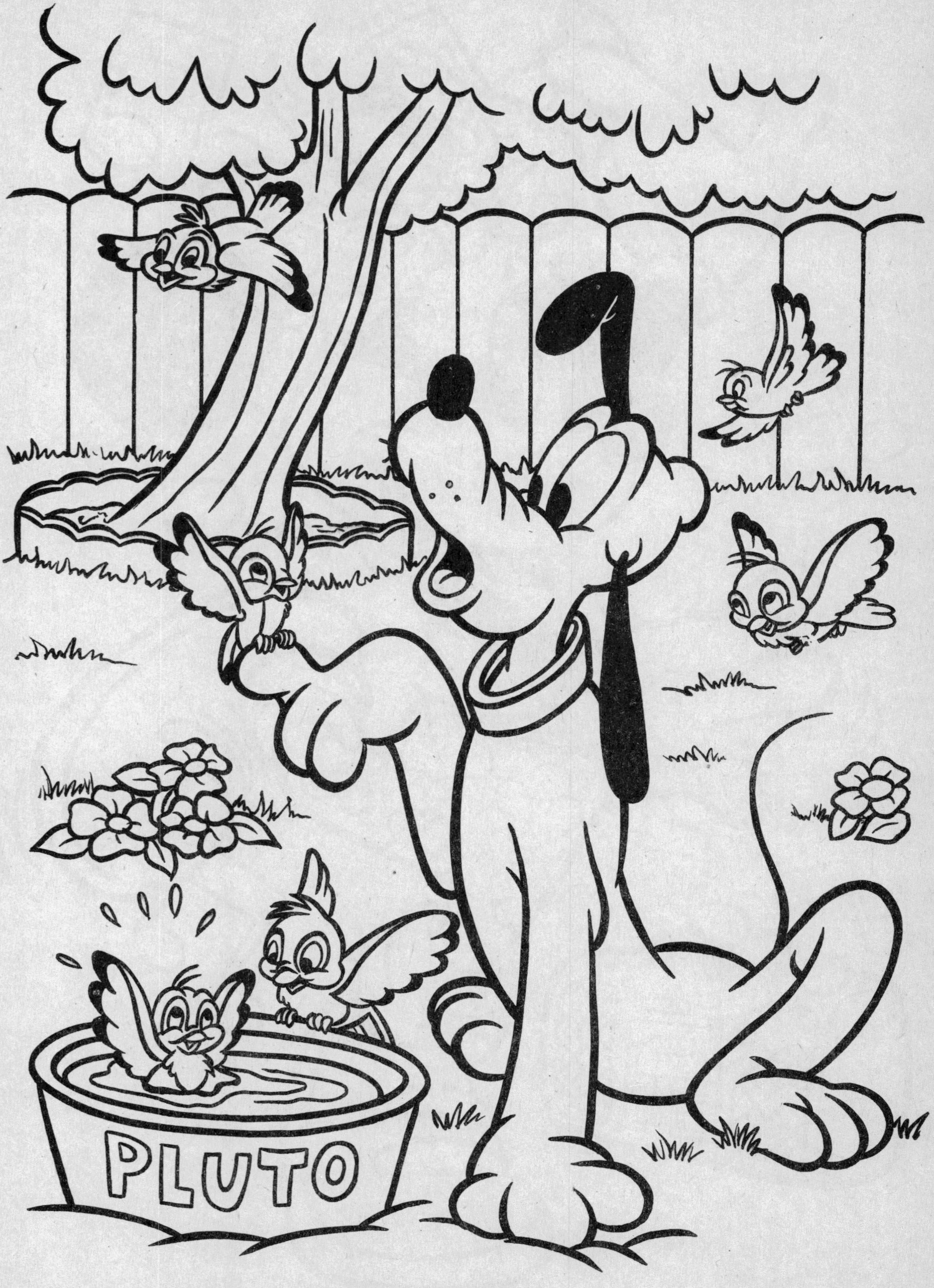
PLUTO

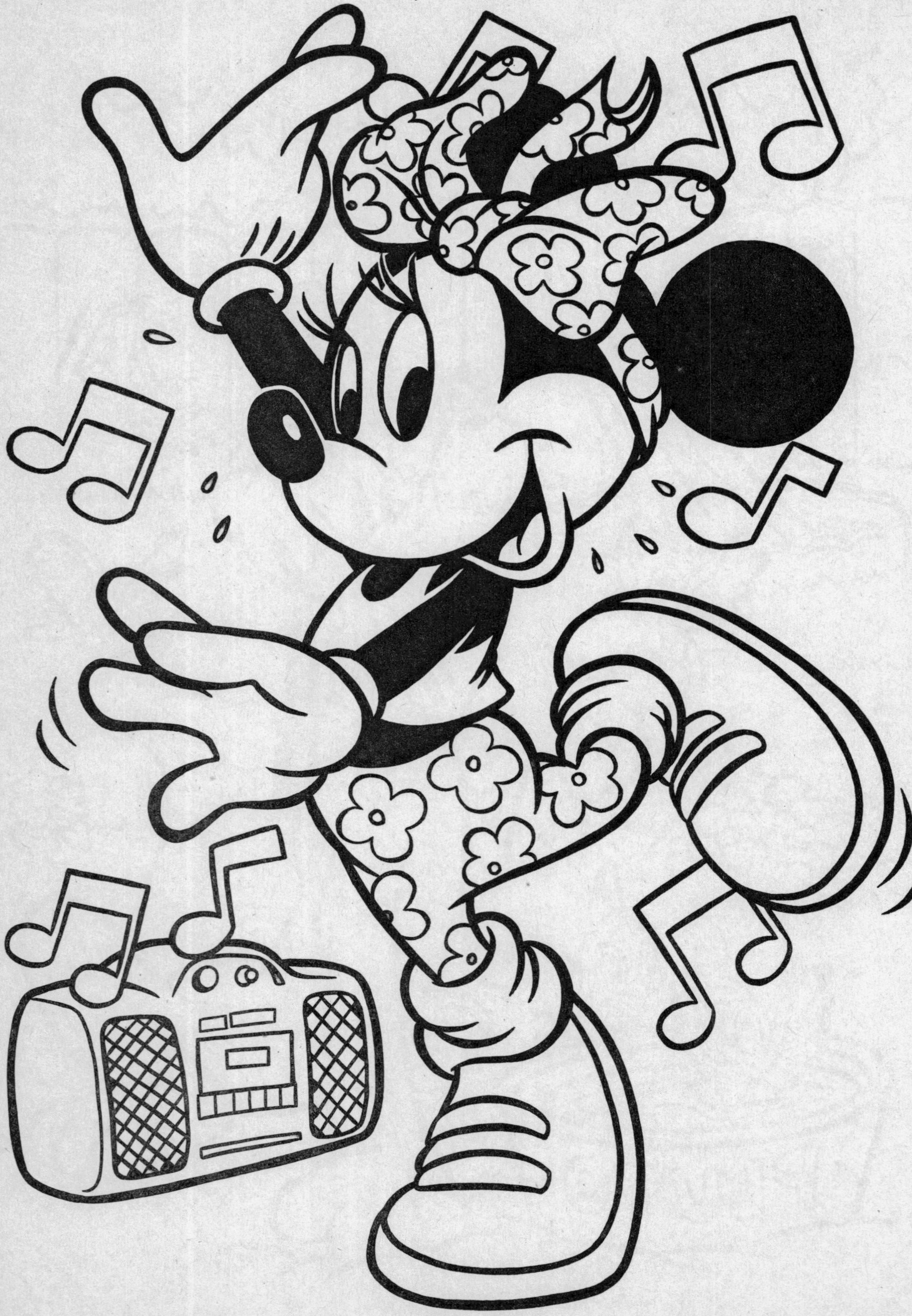

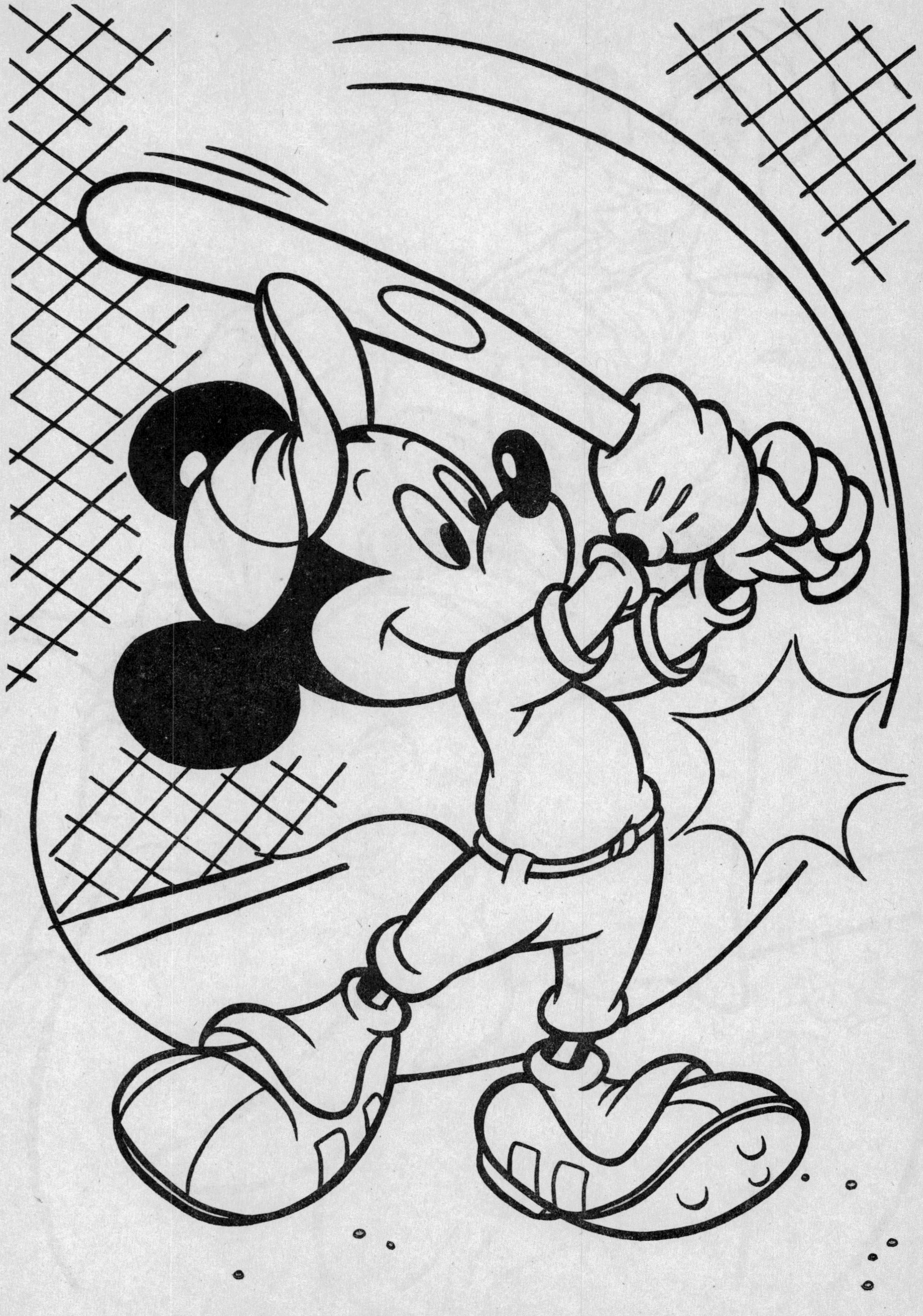

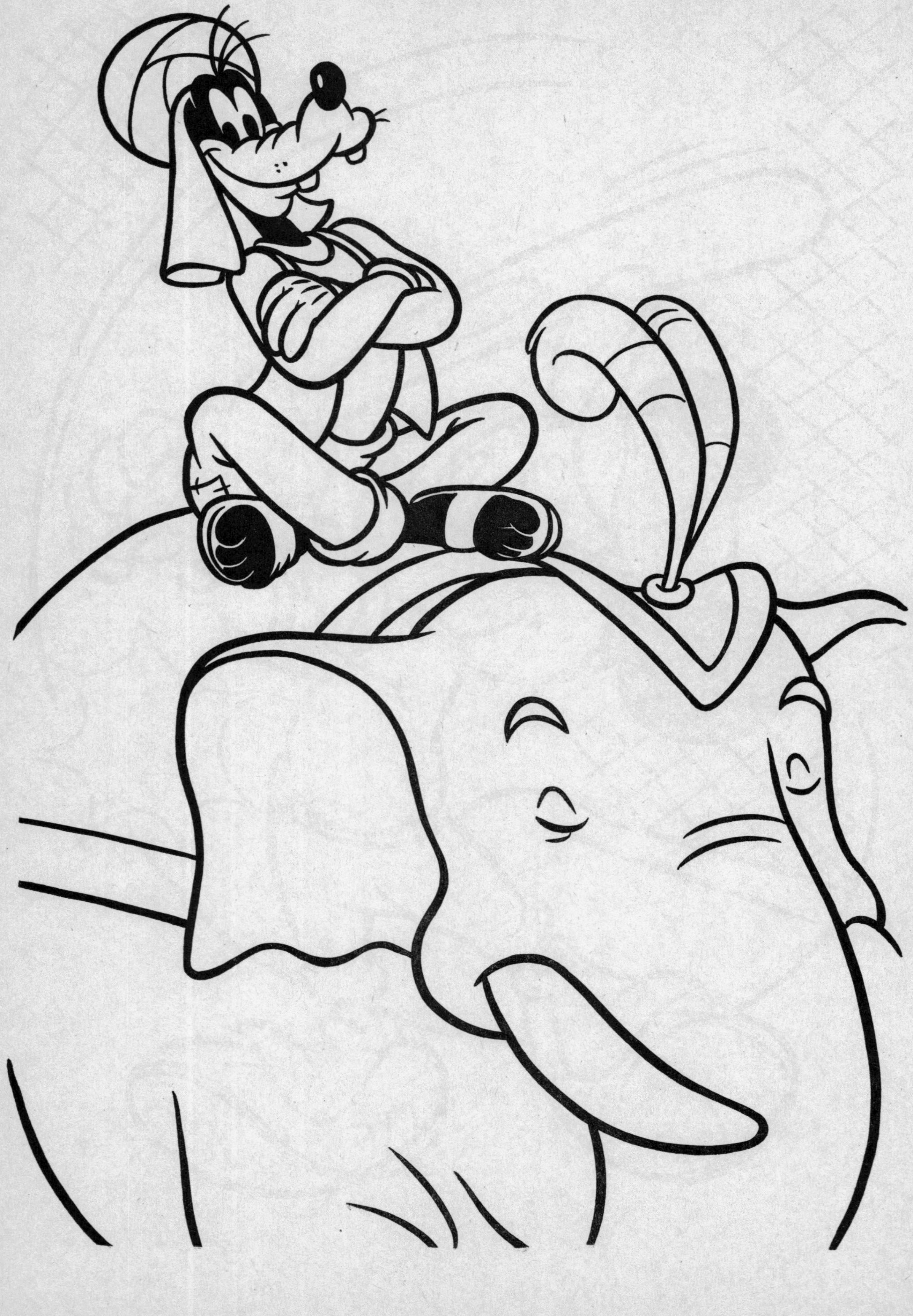

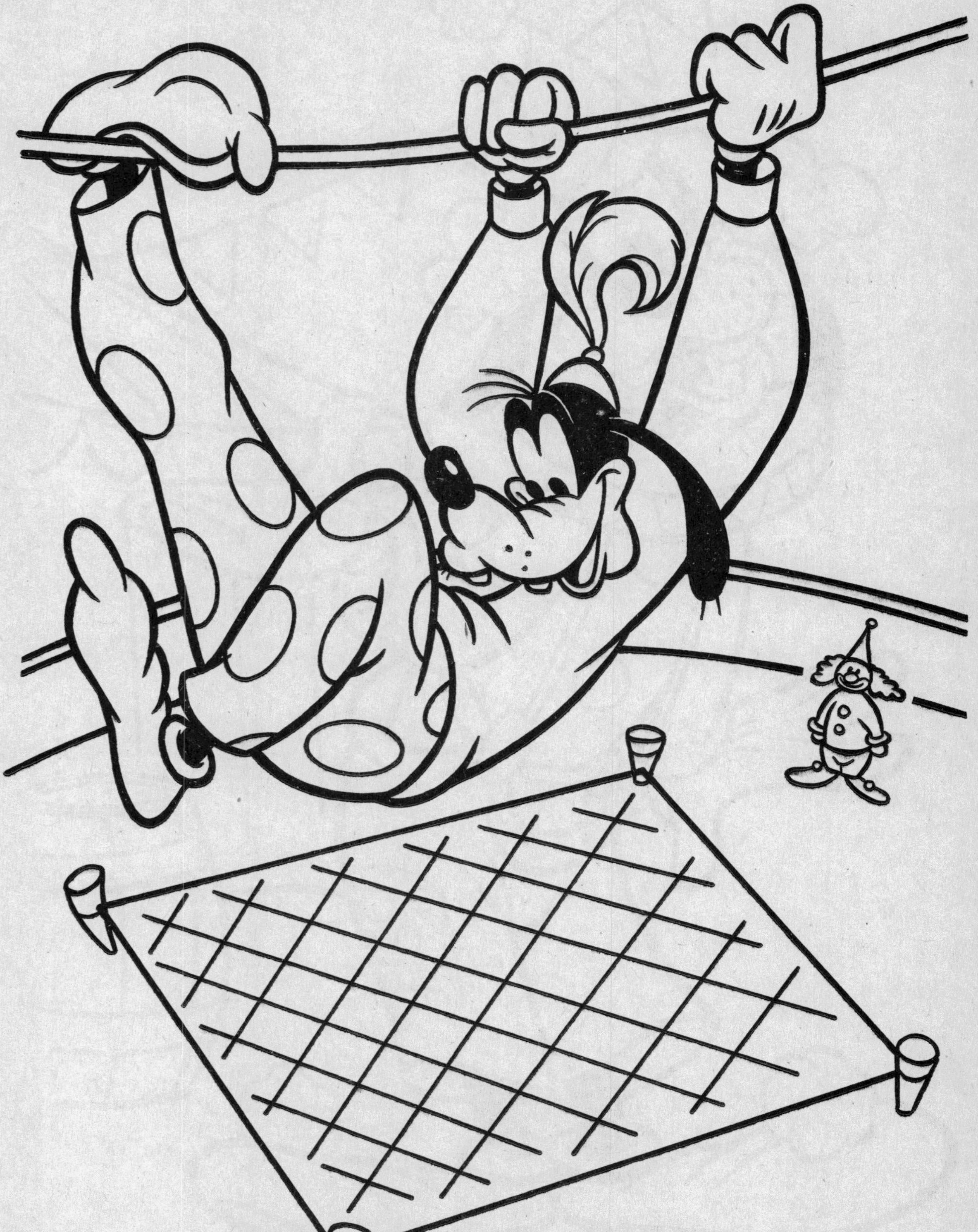

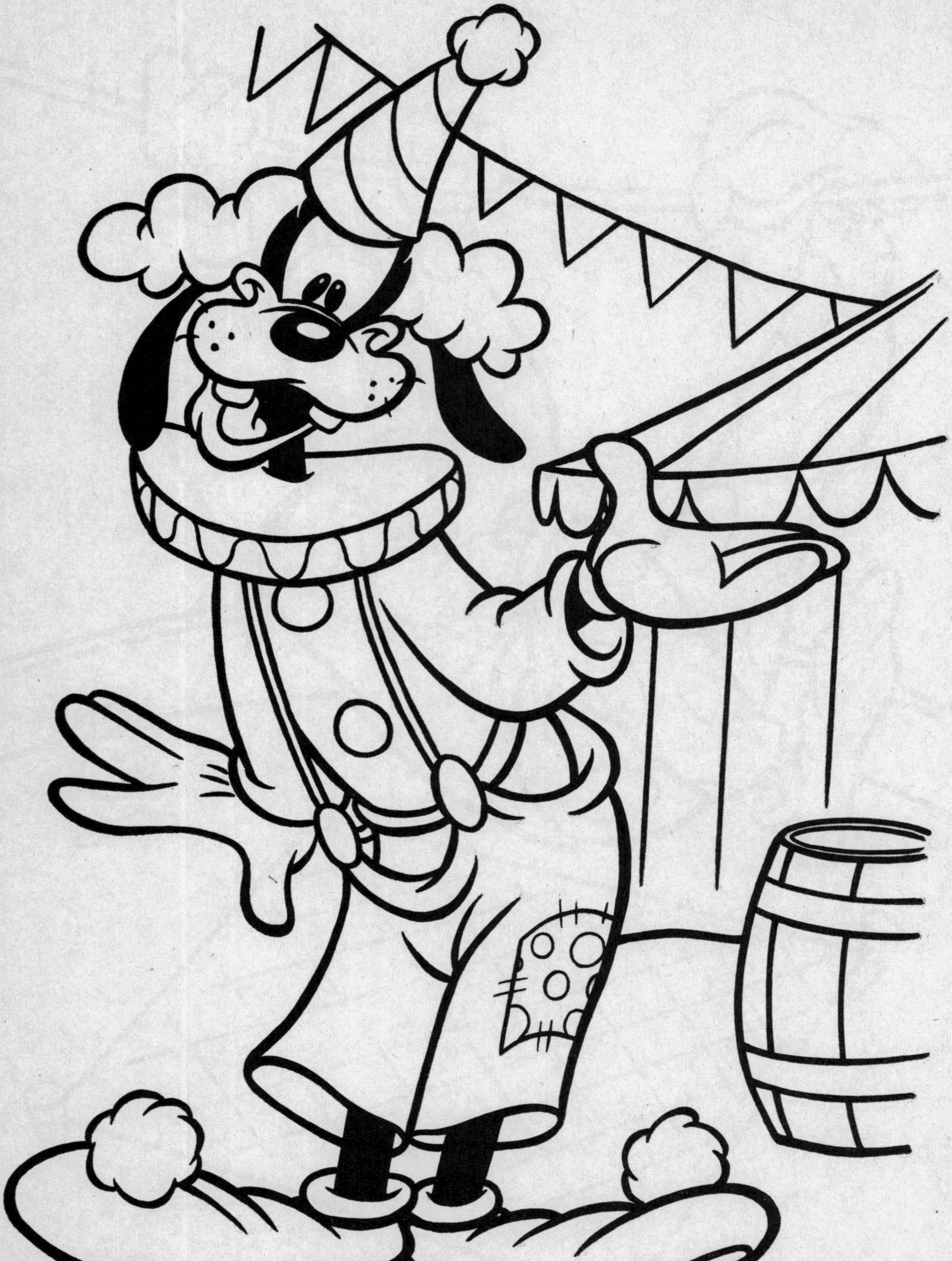

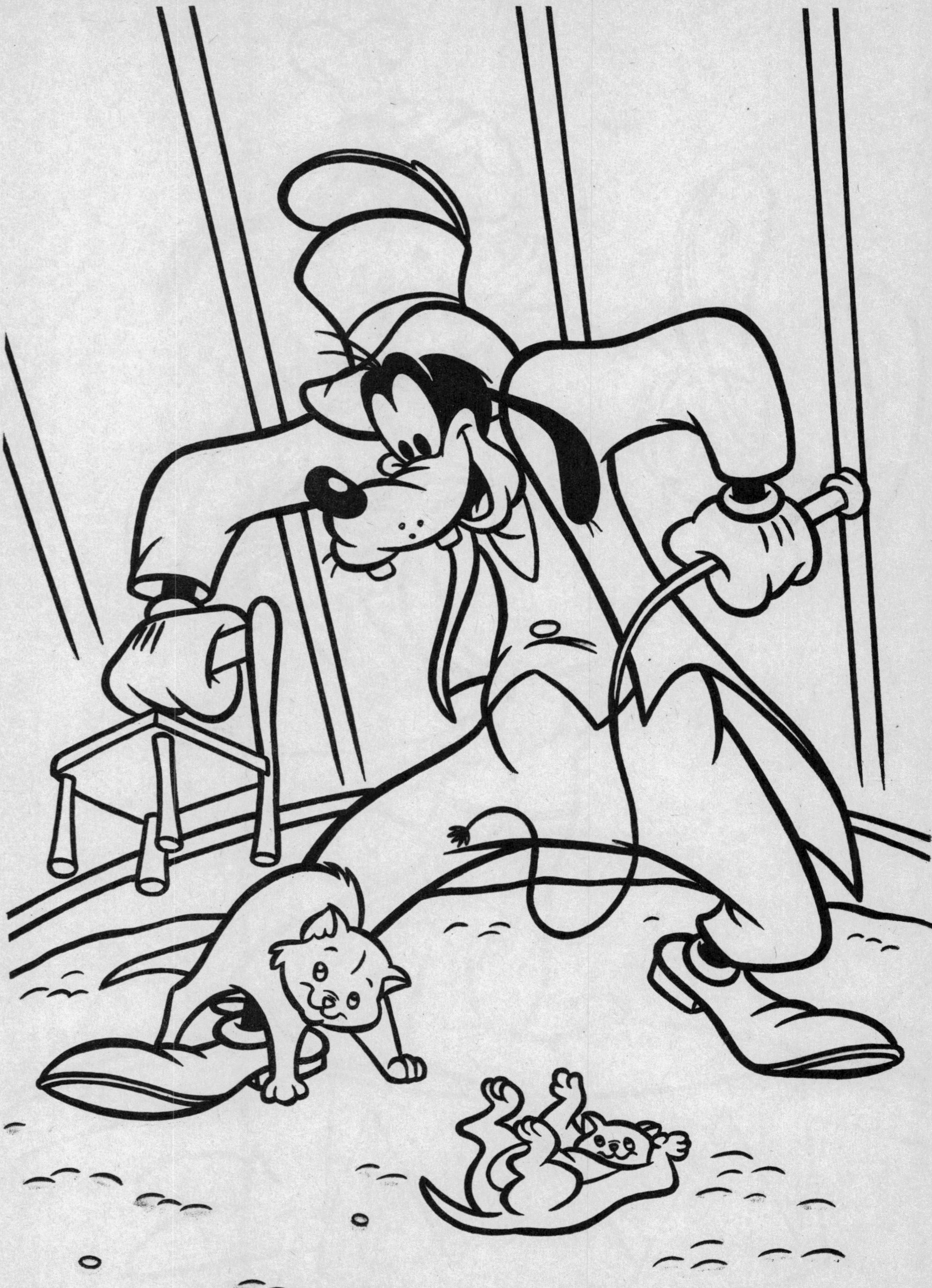

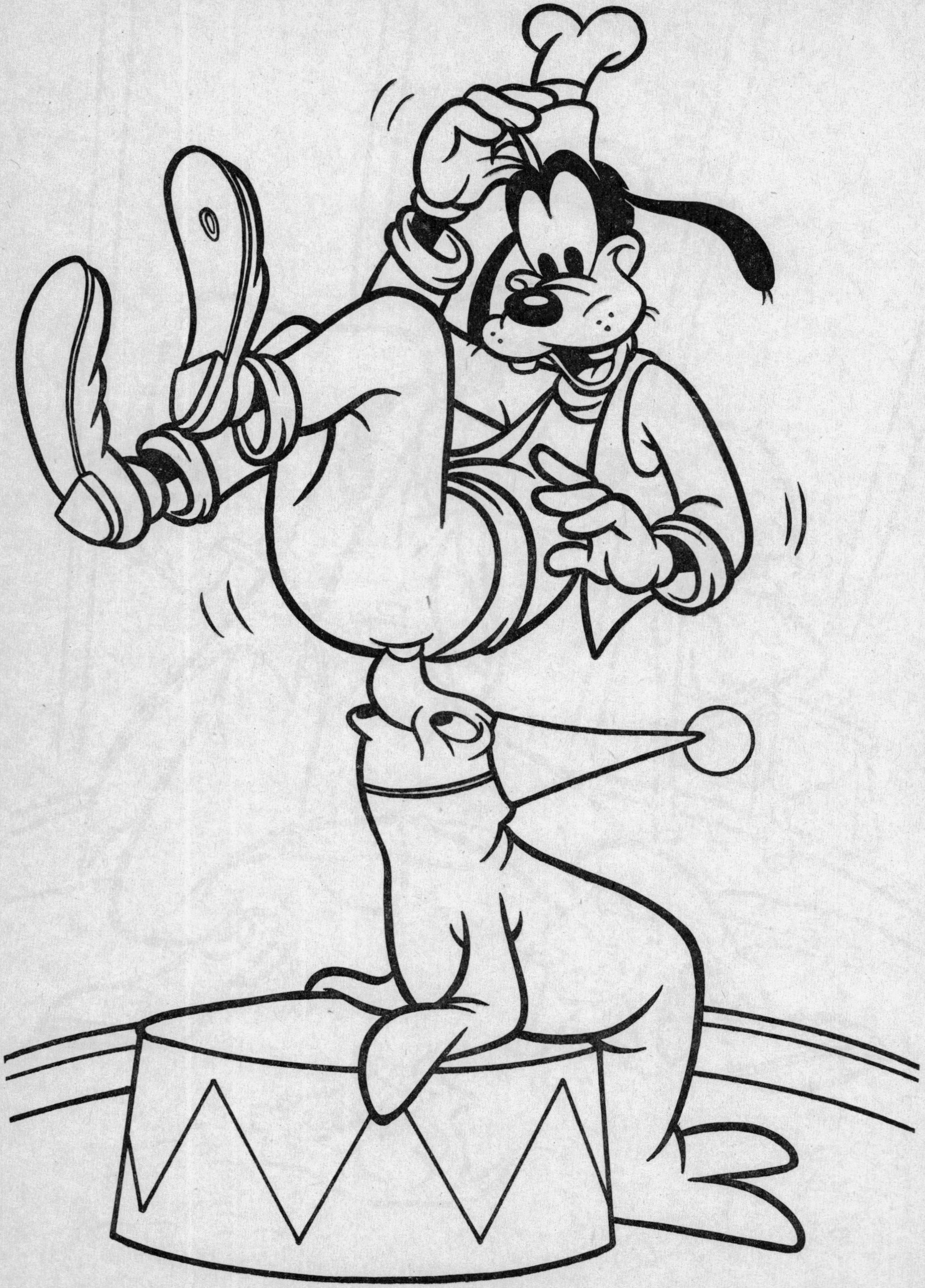

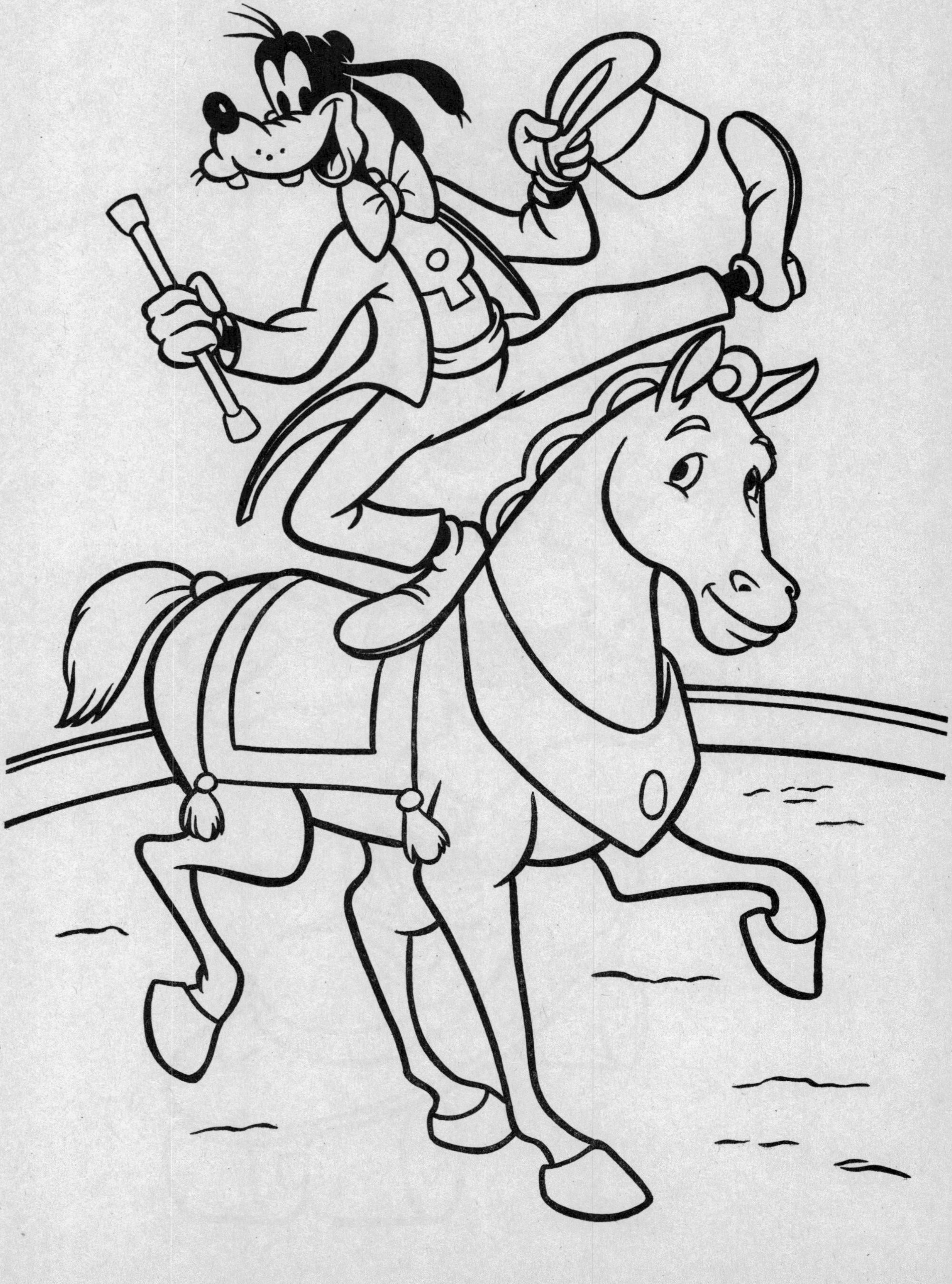

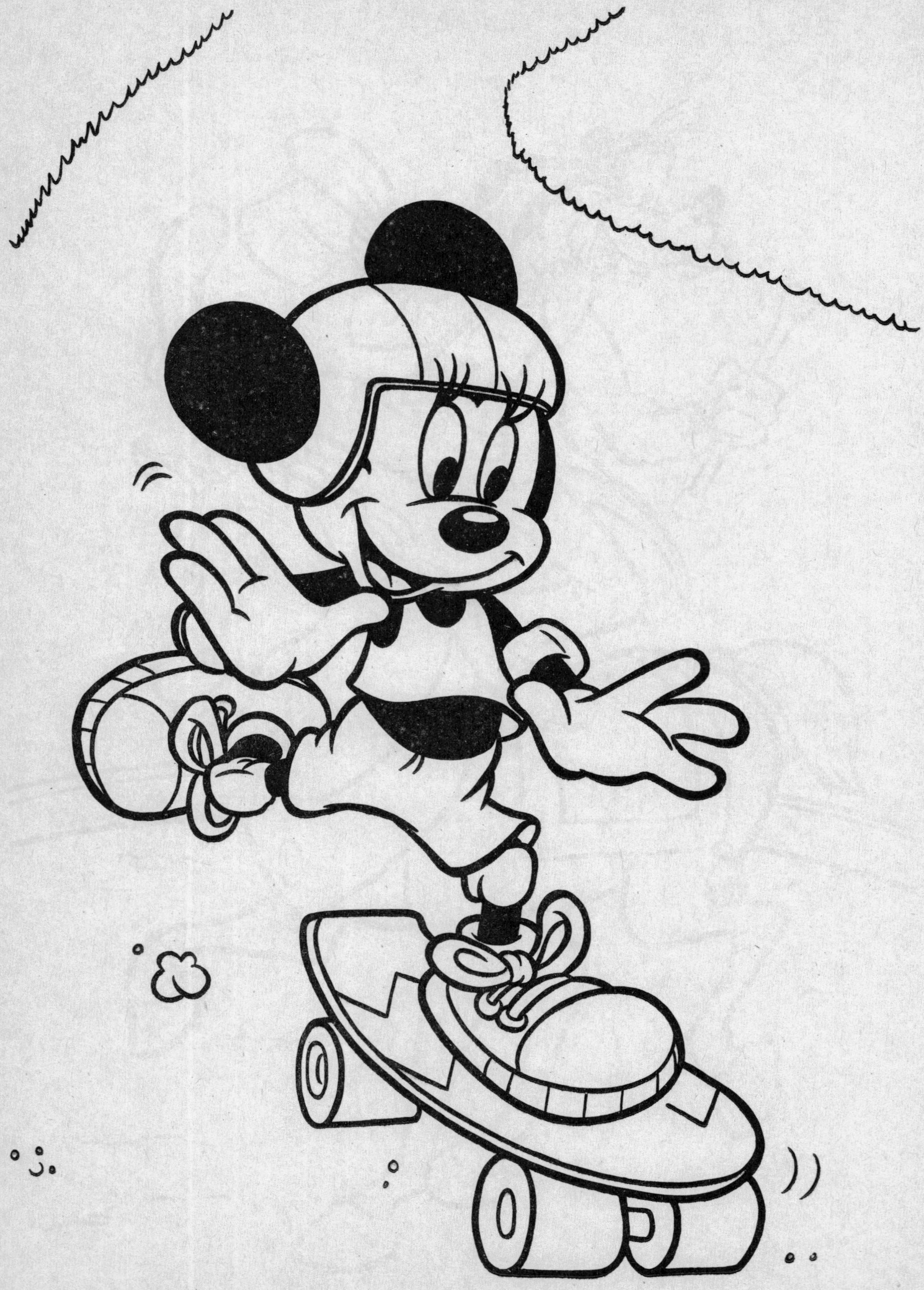

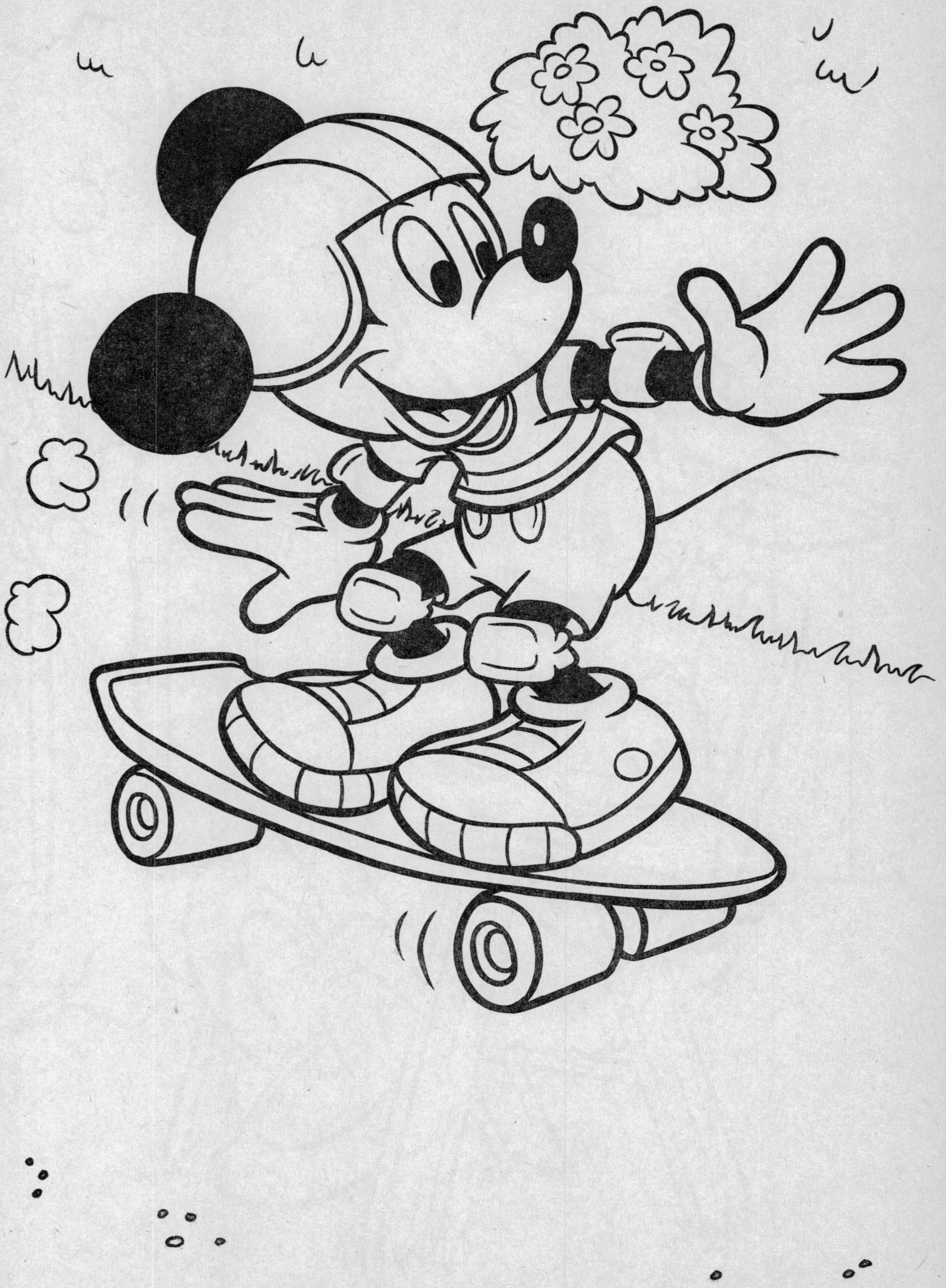

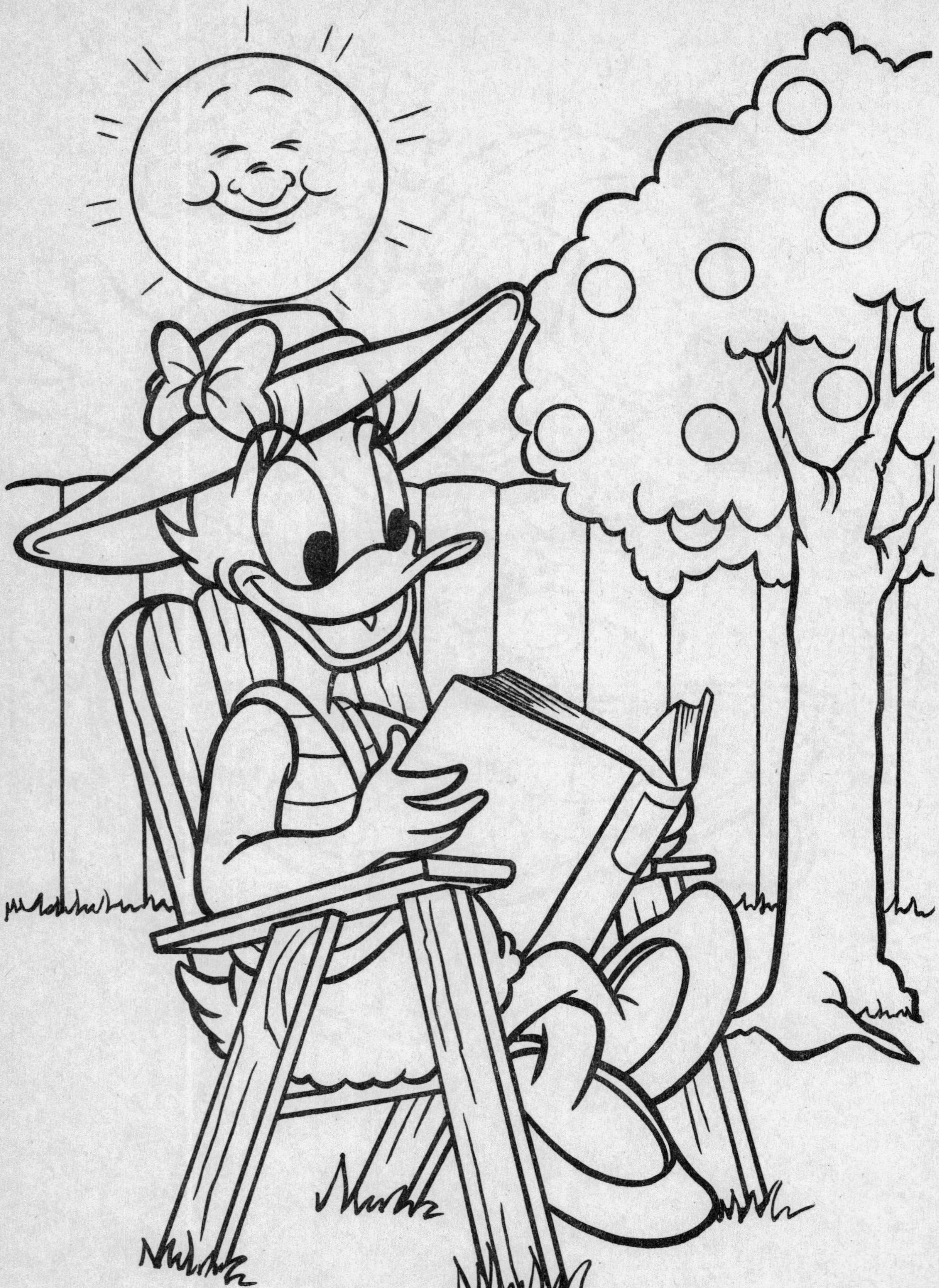

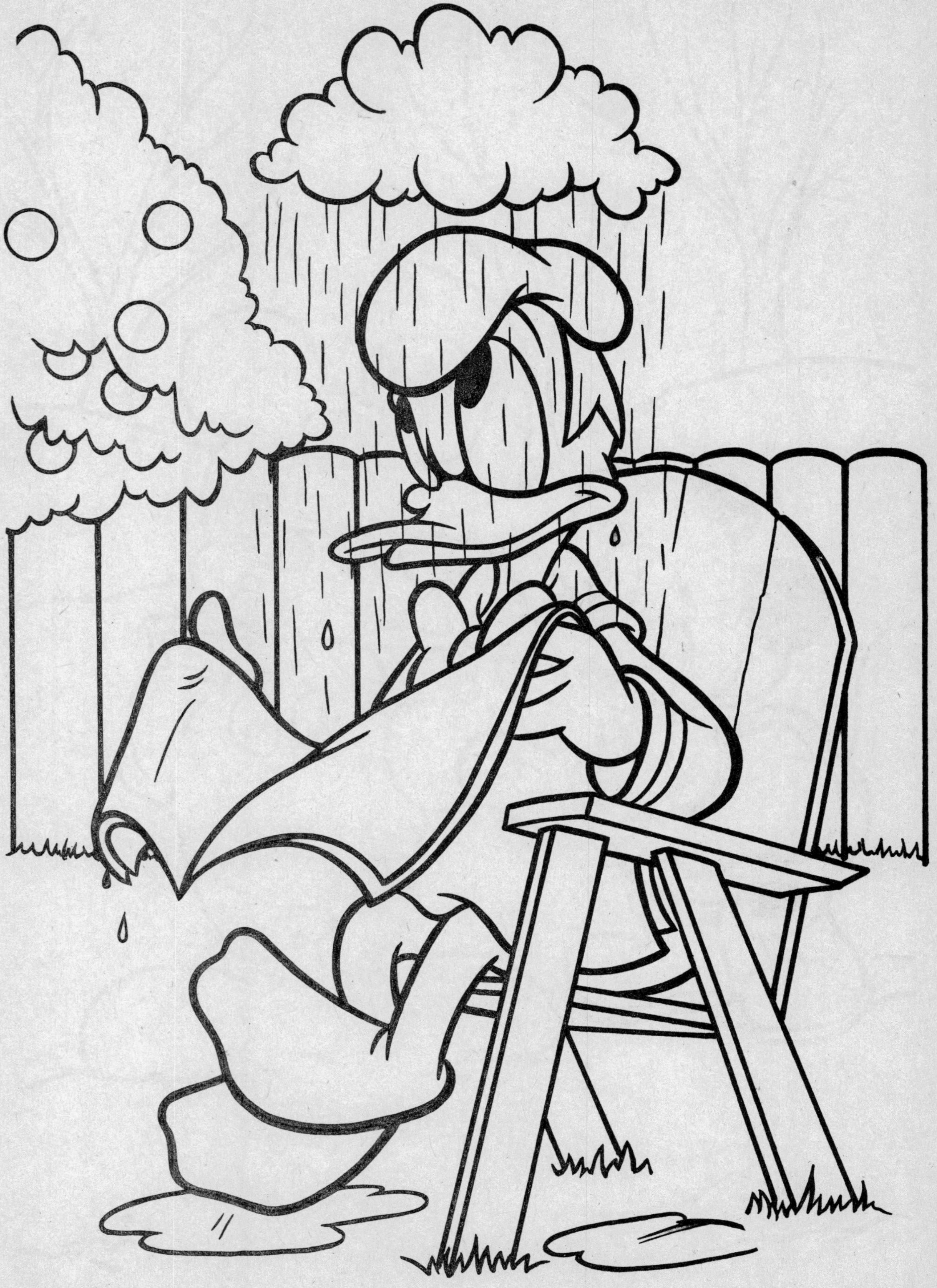

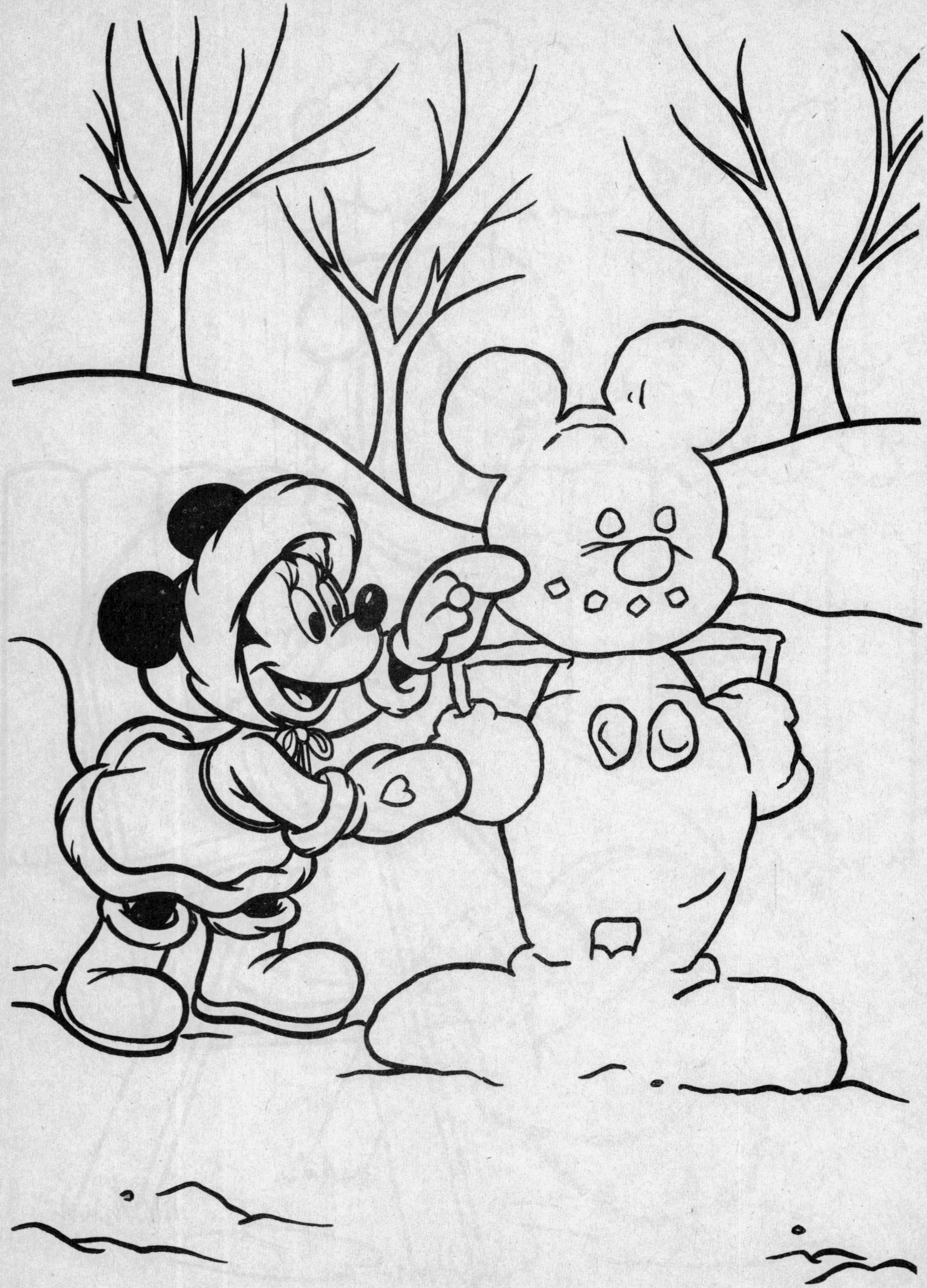

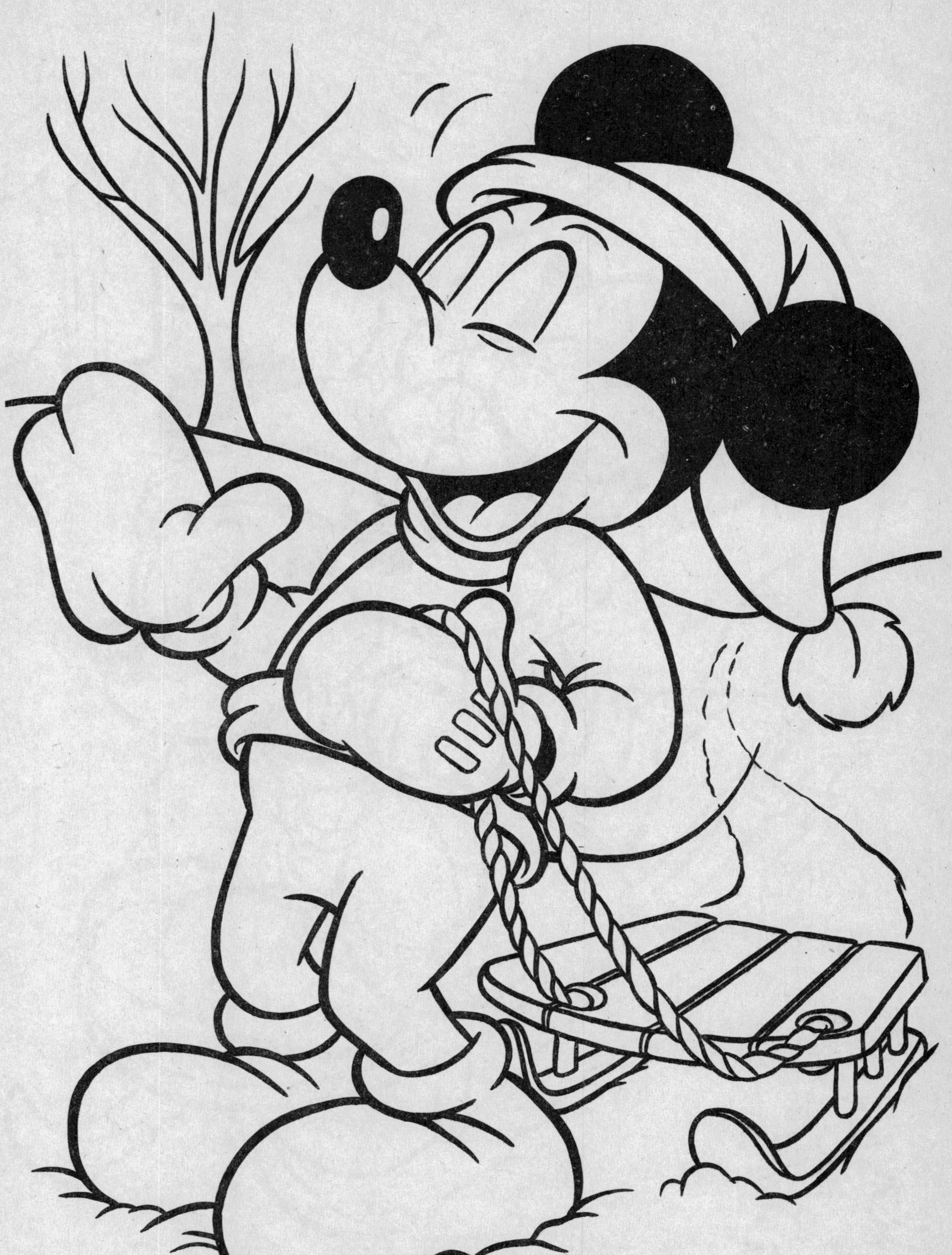

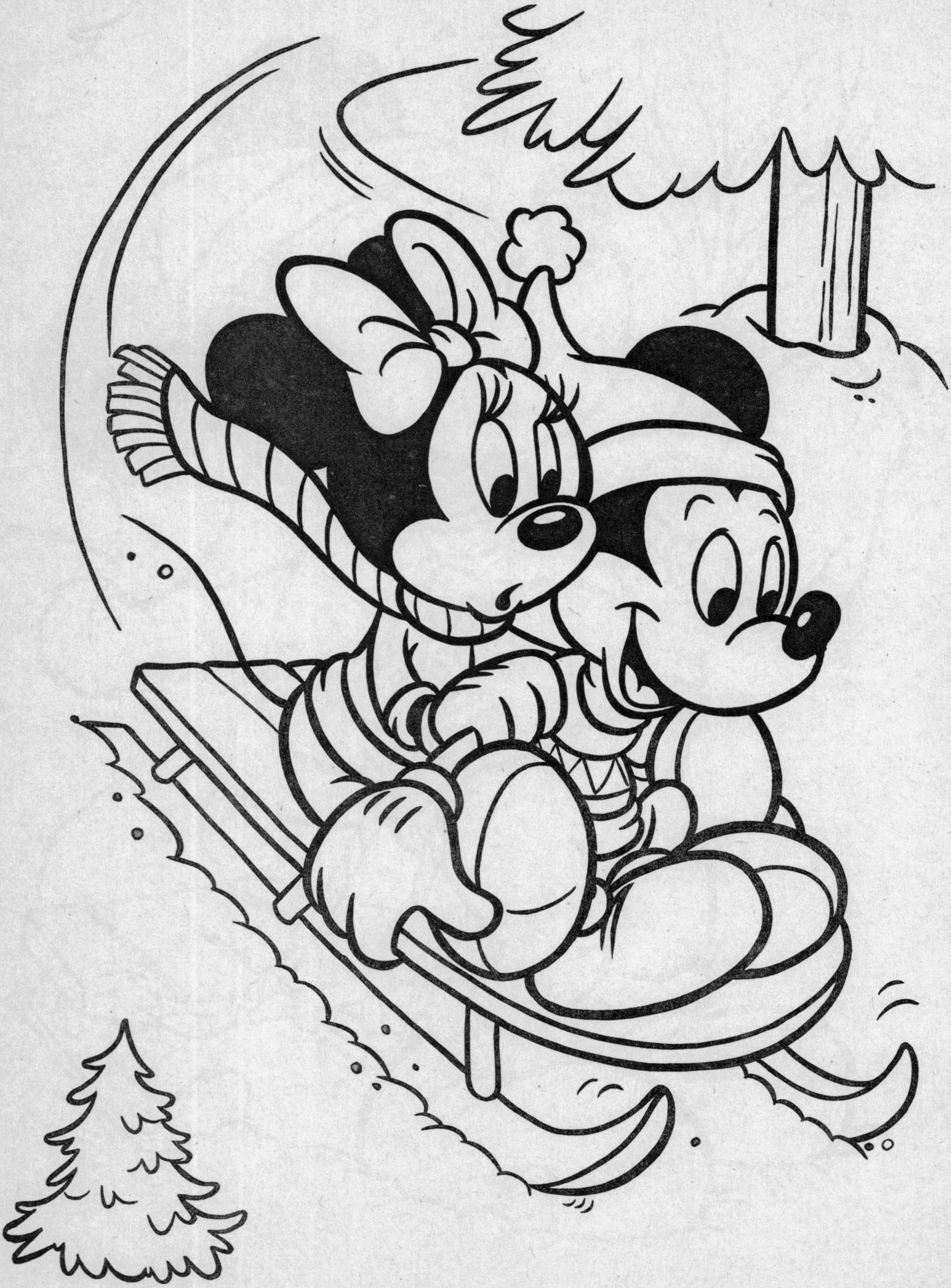

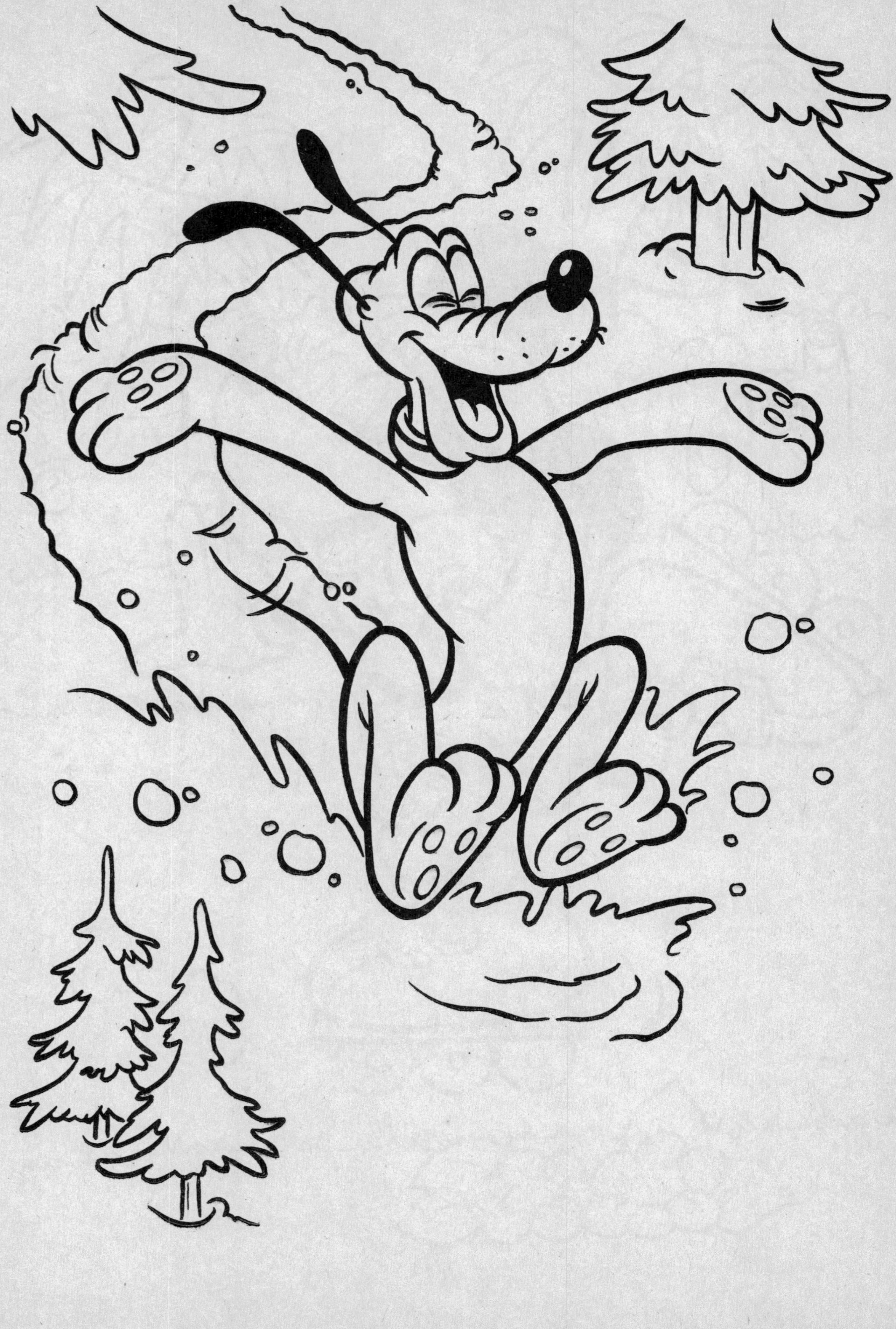

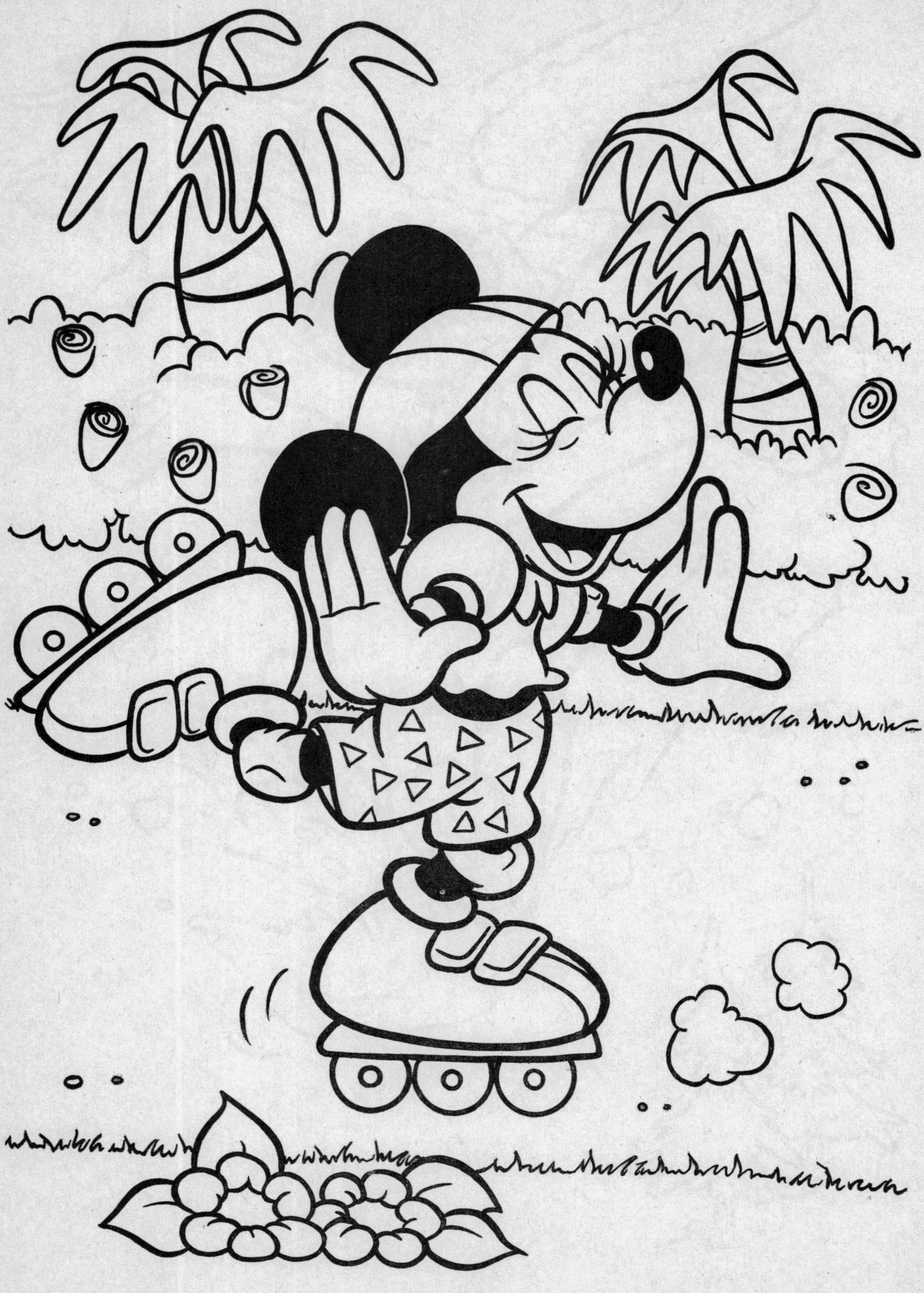

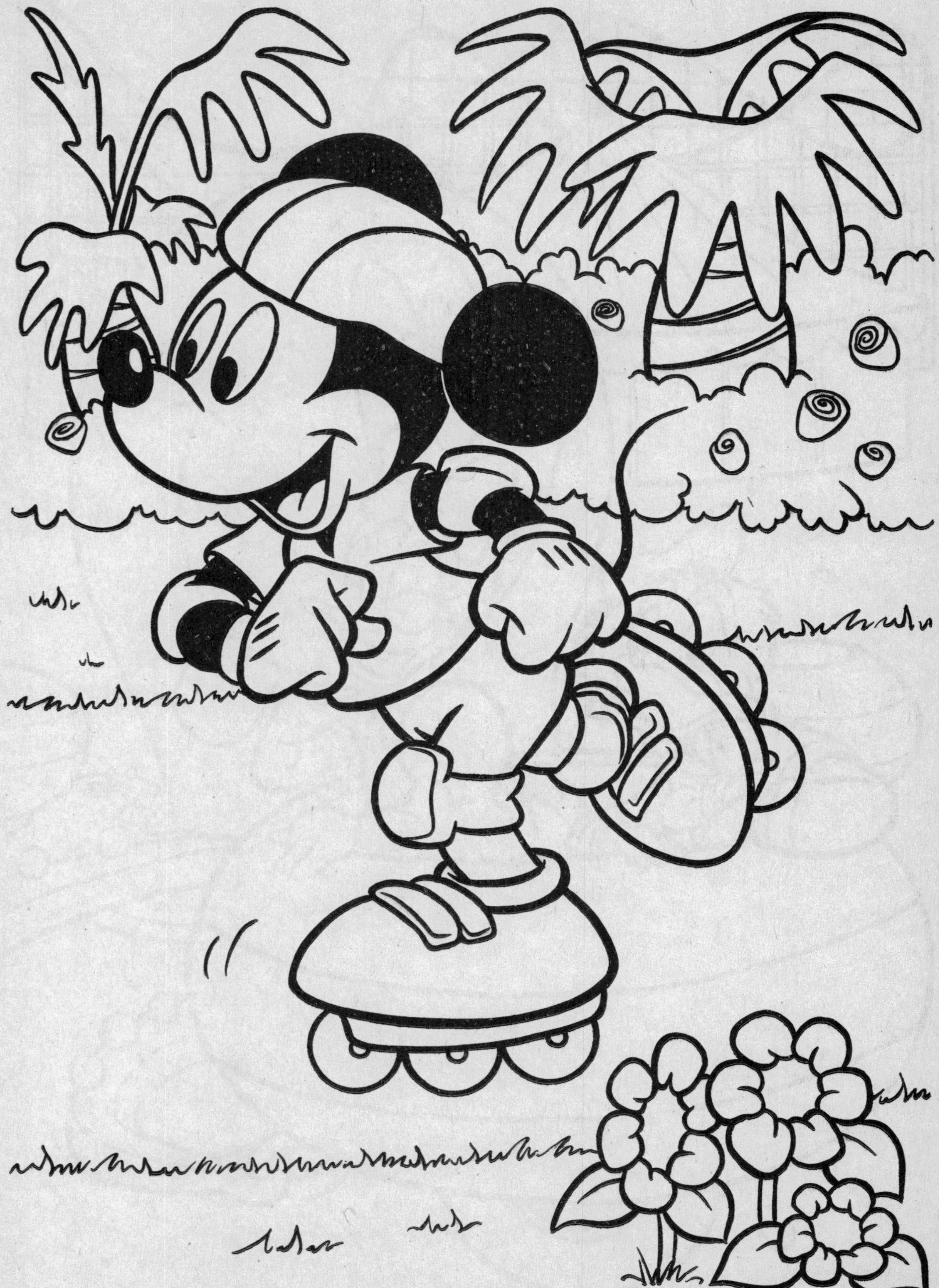

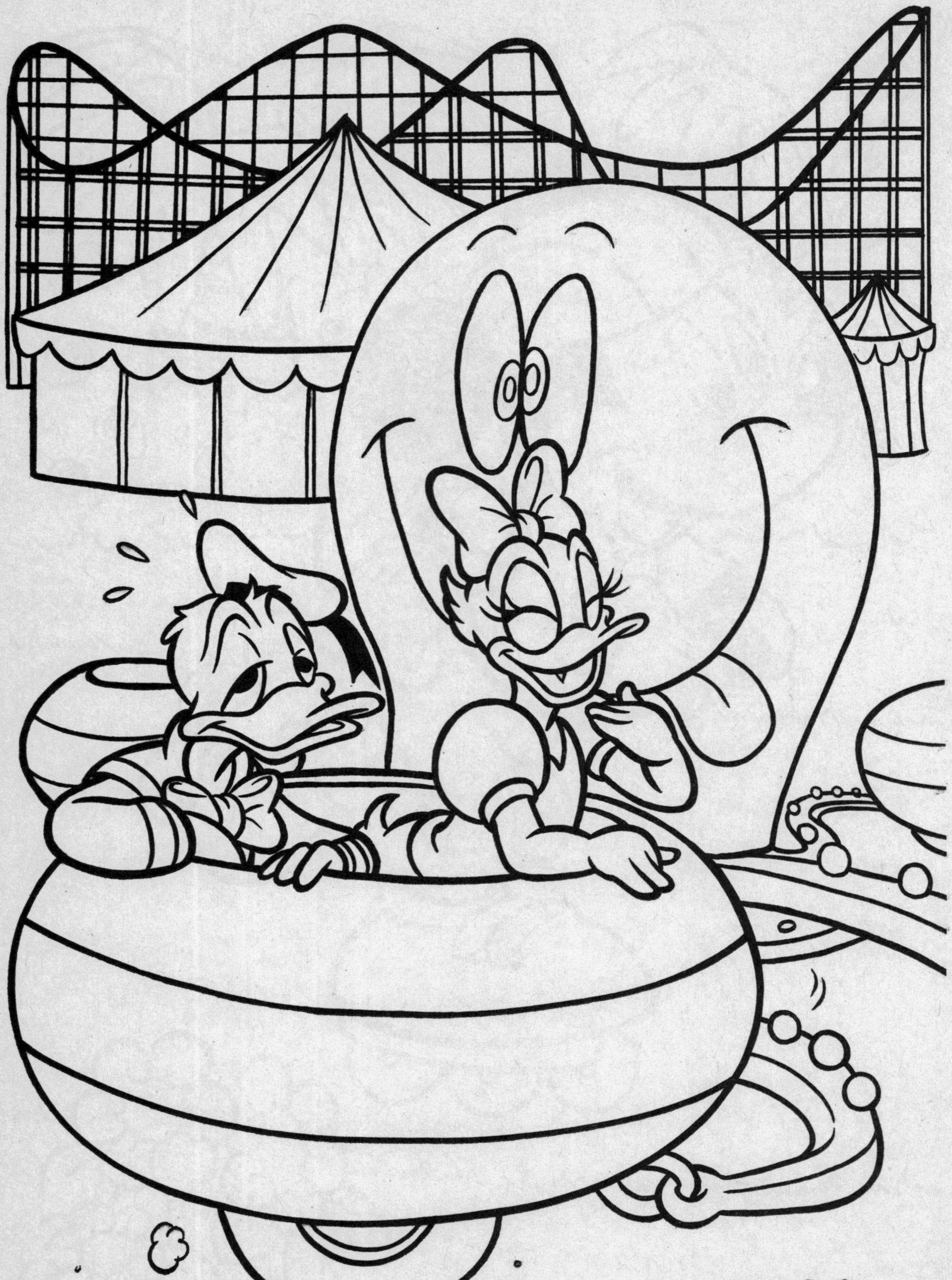

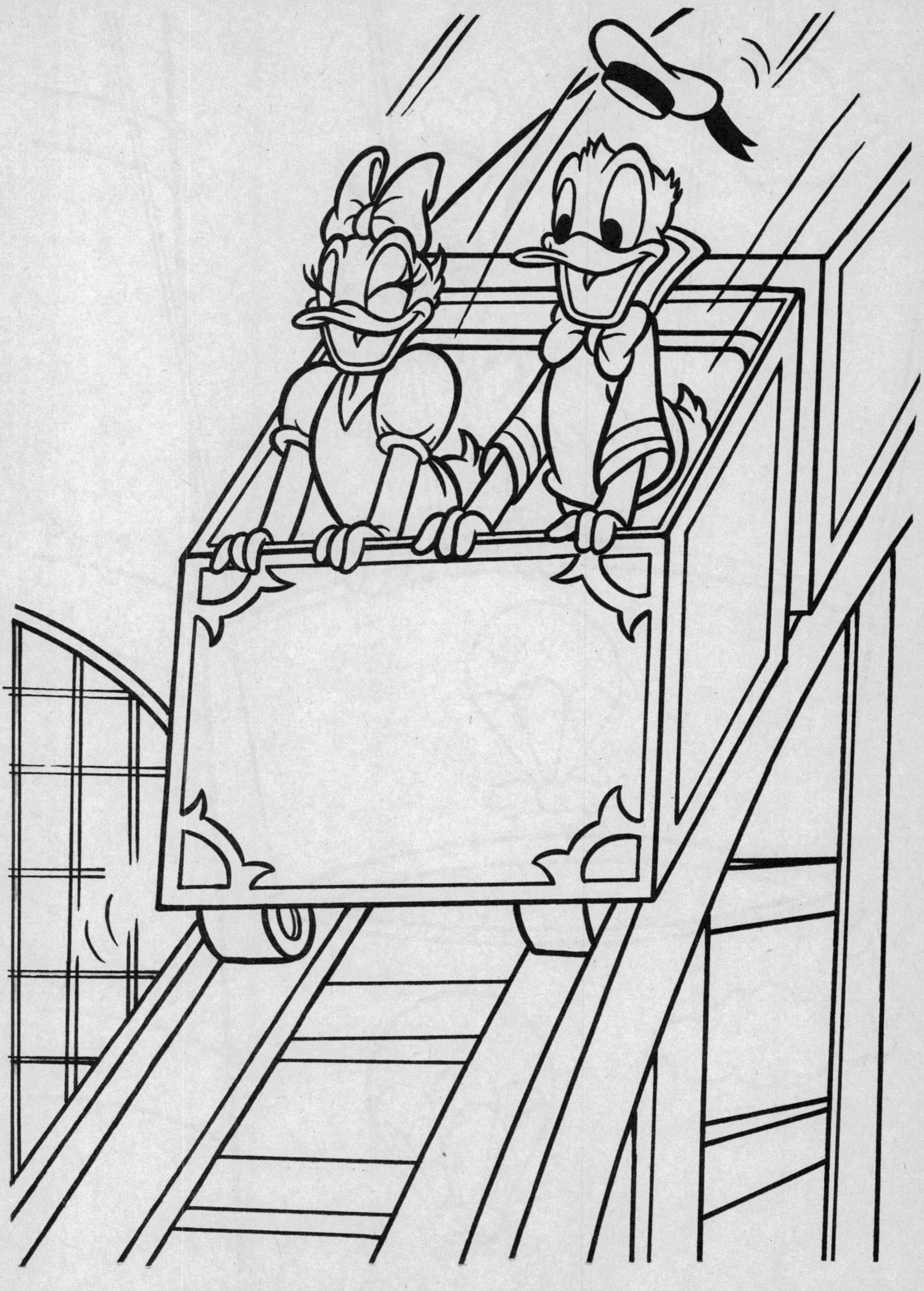

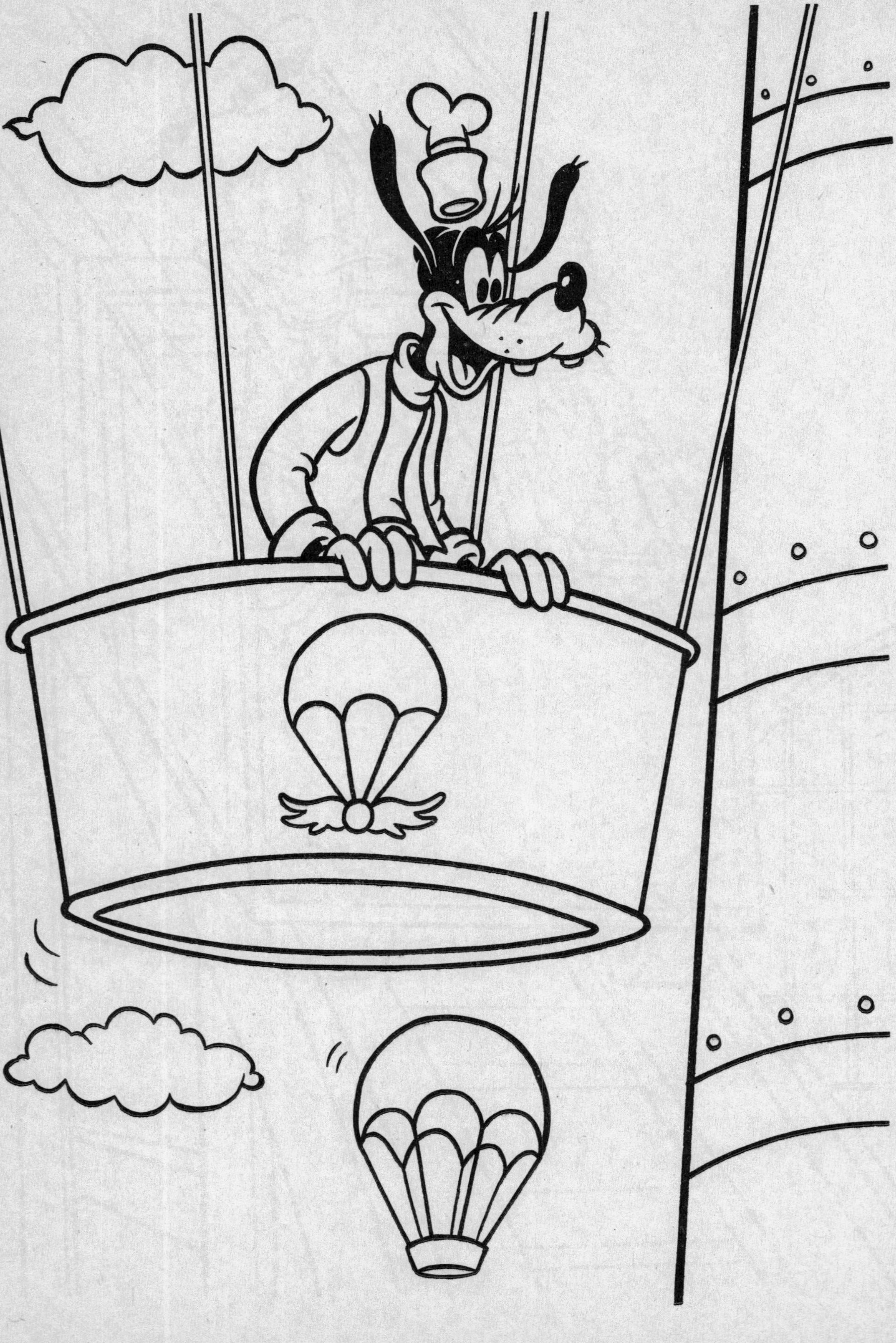

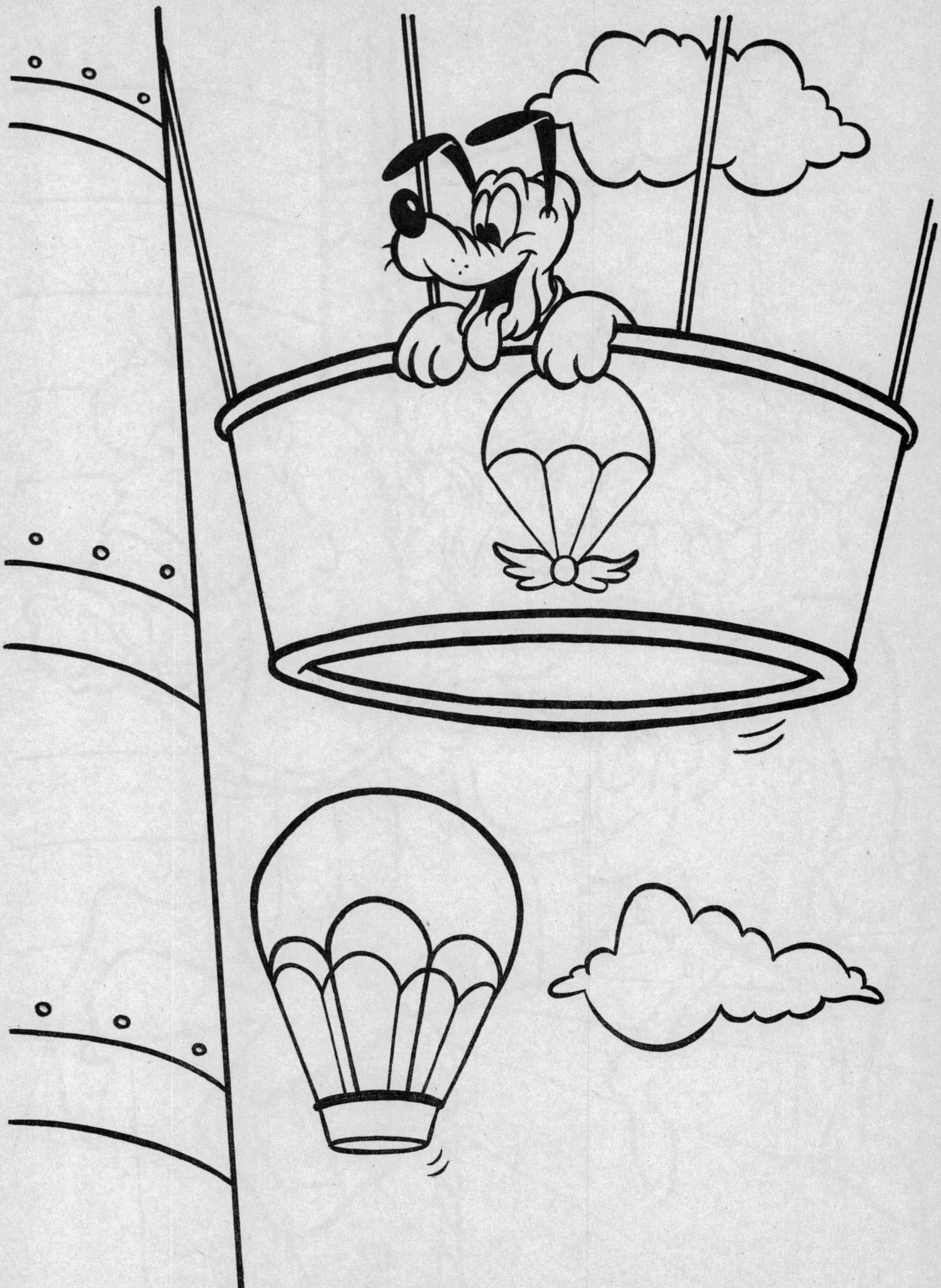

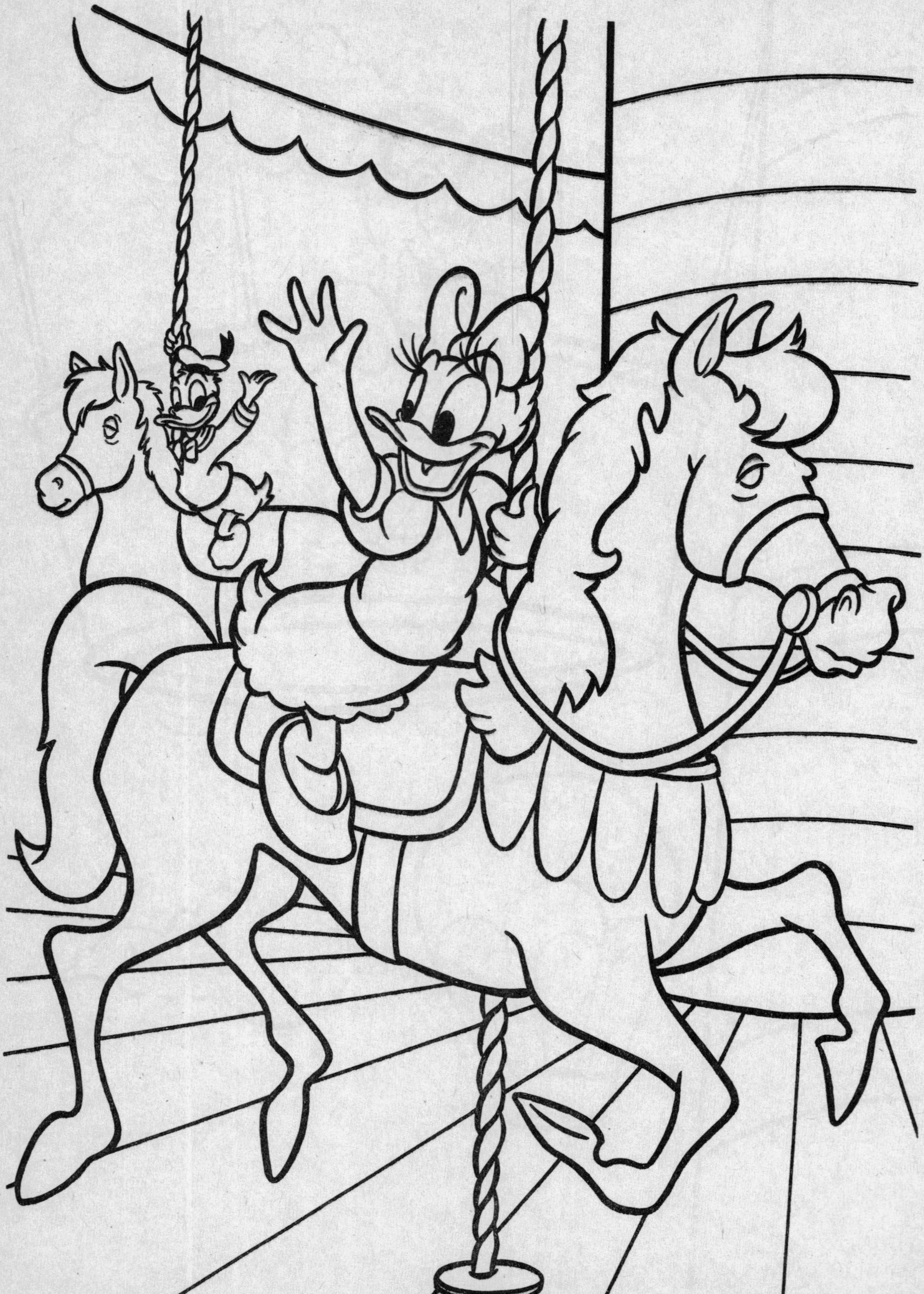

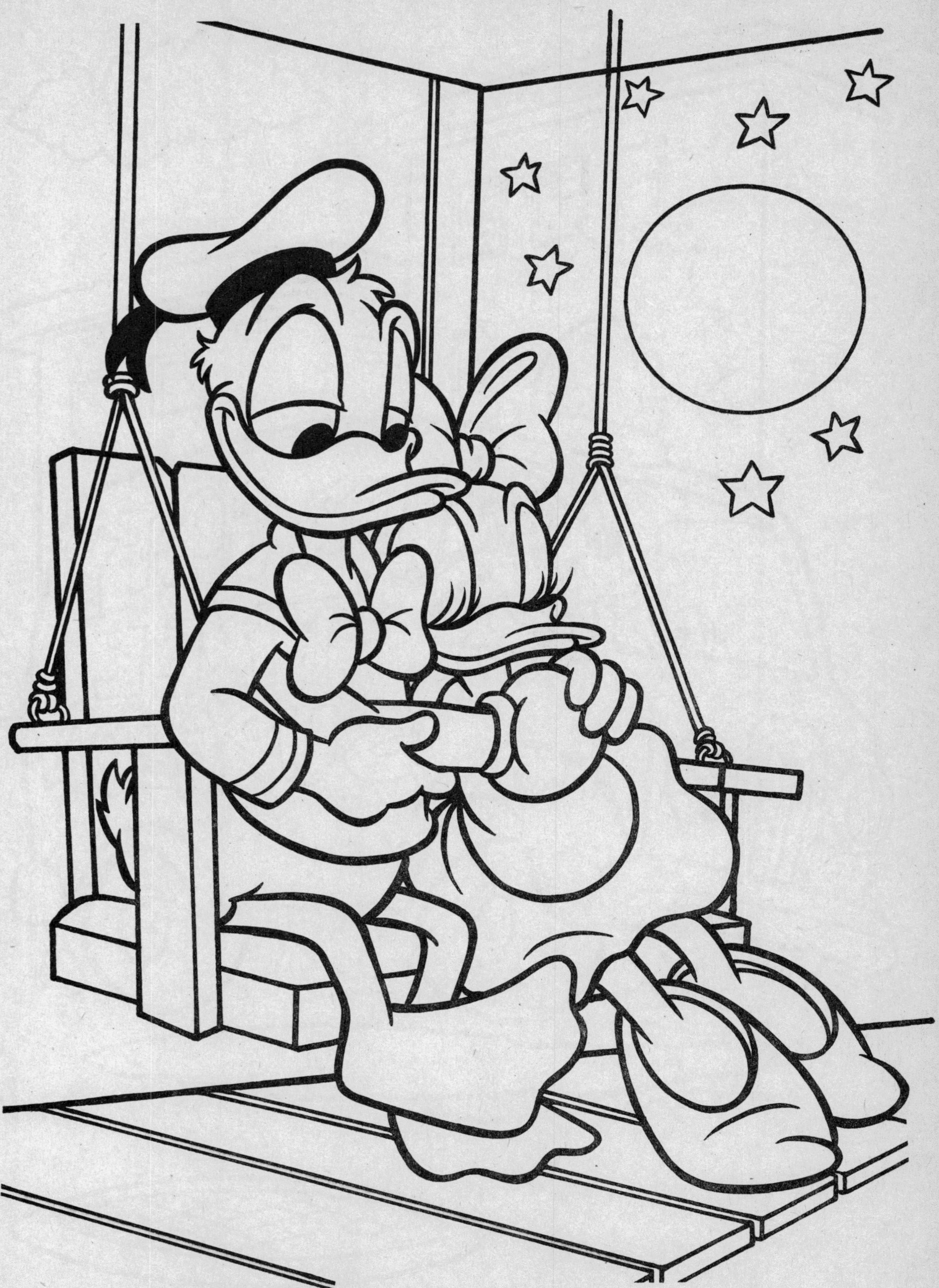

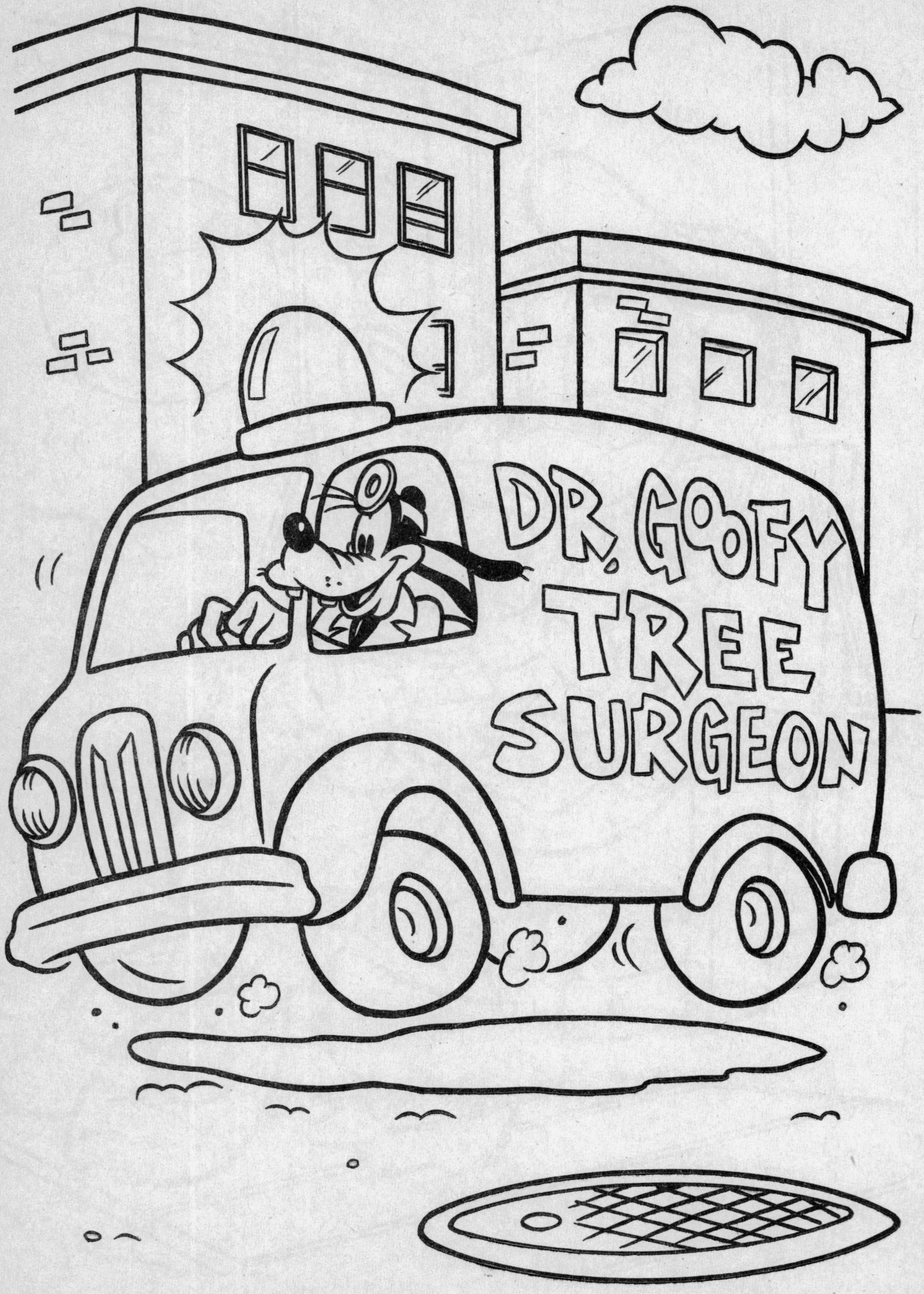
DR. GOOFY
TREE
SURGEON

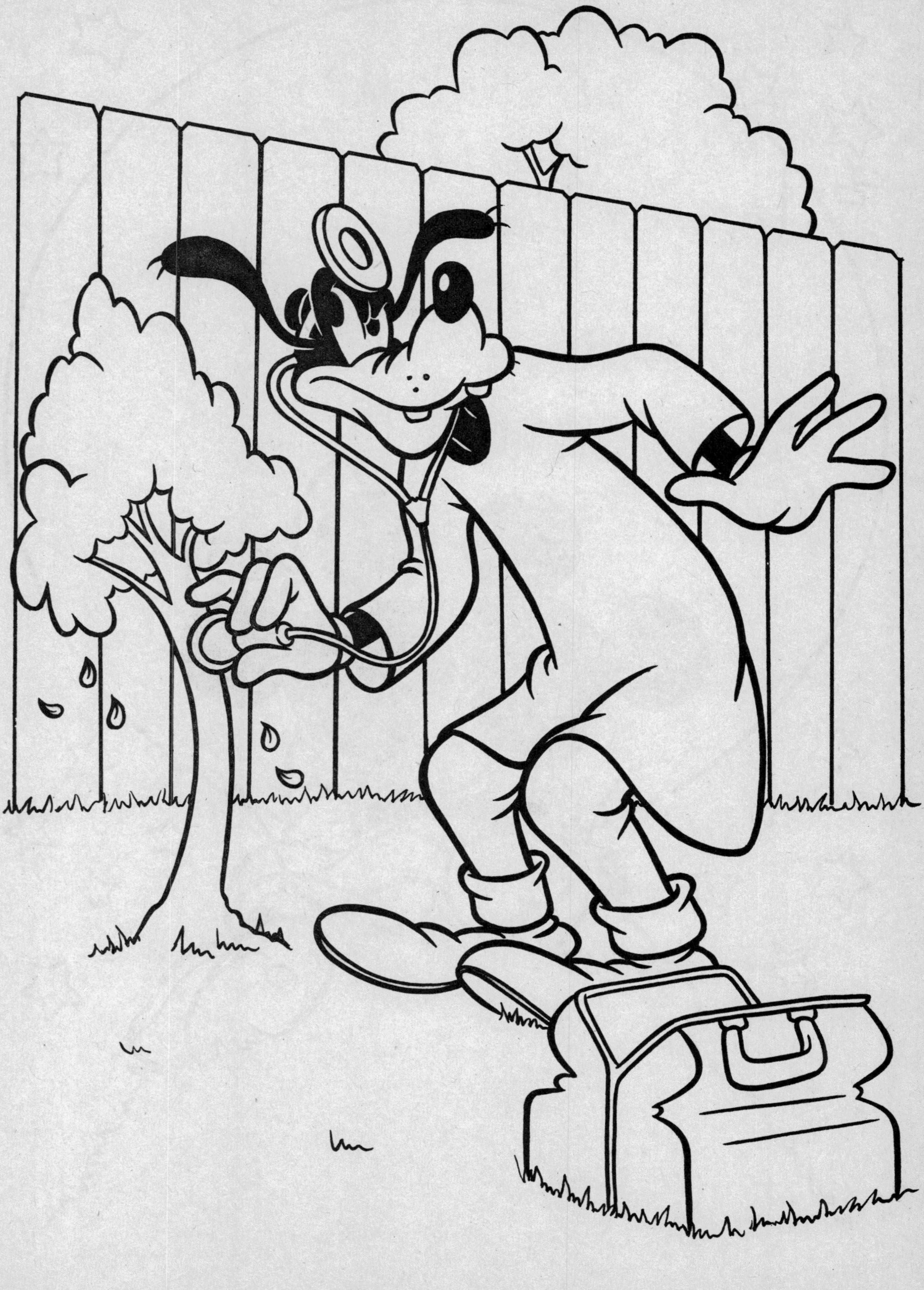

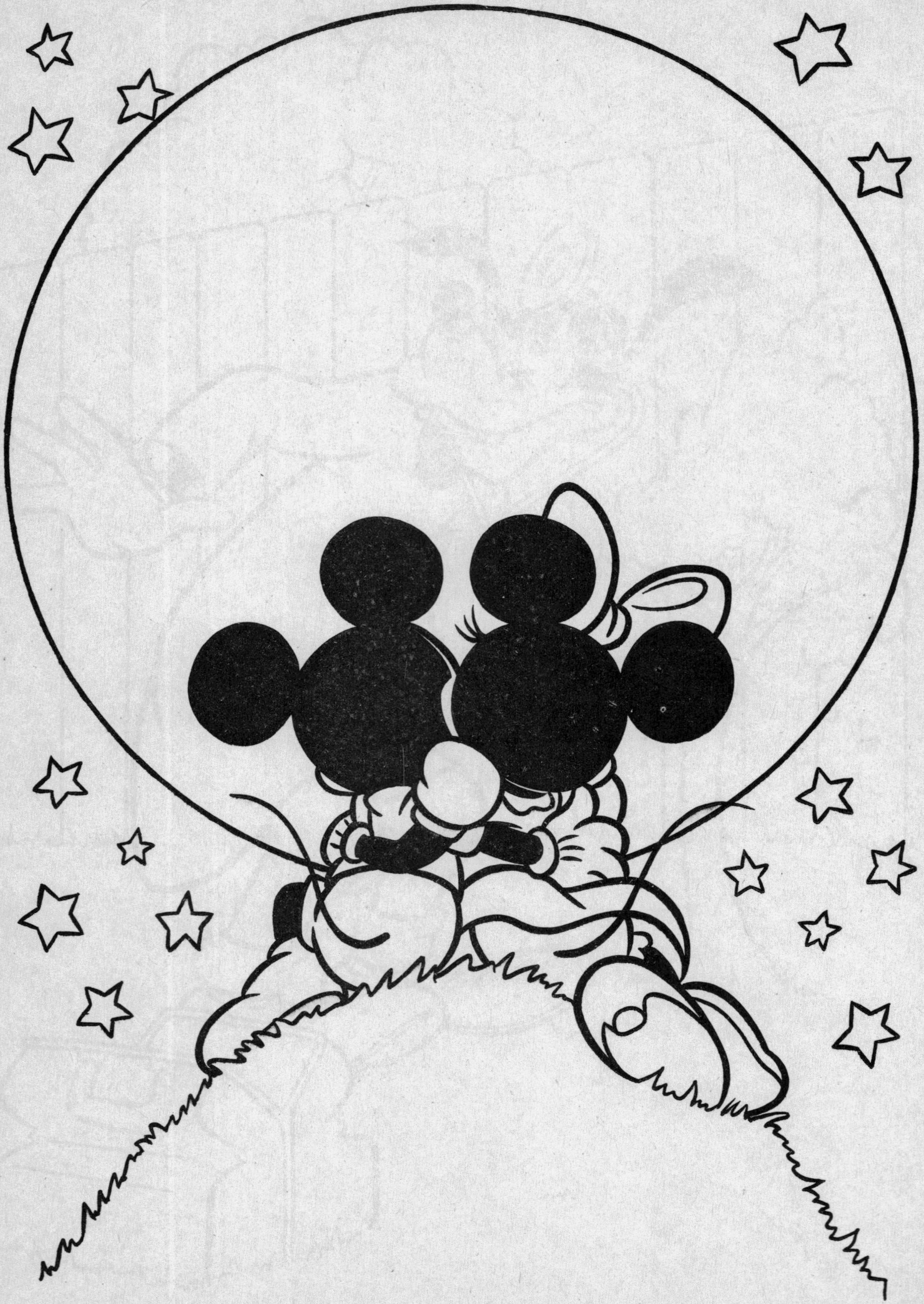